# A Decade of Printmaking

# A Decade of Printmaking

edited by **Charles Spencer**

ACADEMY EDITIONS • LONDON

ST. MARTIN'S PRESS • NEW YORK

The editor and publishers thank the authors and artists for permission to reproduce their work. Also the Editors of *The Times* (London), *Studio International* and *New Society,* and the Arts Council of Great Britain and the British Council, for permission to reprint material.

*Frontispiece:* Editions Alecto's promotional tour of Italy, 1968. Reading from bottom right - Julia Hodgkin, Norbert Lynton, Robert Erskine, Malcolm Billings, Edward Lucie-Smith, Robyn Denny, Anna Denny, David Wainwright, Howard Hodgkin, William Scott, Harry Mundy, Gillian Ayres, Bernard Cohen, José Berlinka, Cliff Hopkinson.

First published in Great Britain in 1973 by Academy Editions,
7 Holland Street, London W8 in association with Editions Alecto Ltd.

First published in the U.S.A. in 1973 by St. Martin's Press Inc.,
175 Fifth Avenue, New York, N.Y. 10010.
Affiliated publishers: Macmillan Company Limited, London -also at
Bombay, Calcutta, Madras and Melbourne - The Macmillan Company
of Canada Limited, Toronto.

Printed in Great Britain by Burgess & Son (Abingdon) Ltd.

# CONTENTS

# David Hockney

A Rake's Progress and Other Etchings

4 to 24 December 1963

Daily 10 am to 6 pm   Saturdays 10 am to 2 pm

Editions Alecto   The Print Centre   8 Holland Street   London W 8

---

Artists from

# ATELIER 17

Etchings

14 April to 23 May 1964

Daily 10am to 6pm Saturdays 10am to 2pm

Editions Alecto The Print Centre 8 Holland Street London W8

---

 **new graphics from Editions Alecto at the Atelier Chapman Kelley Dallas**

Previewing May 17-18, 5-8 P.M.
Exhibition May 17-23, 1969

---

The Hypnotist

Britische Graphische Scene 1963

---

The directors of Editions Alecto Limited
invite you to an Apolitical Election Night Party
at which their new publications

Eduardo Paolozzi's
**GENERAL DYNAMIC F.U.N.**

Ed Ruscha's
**News, Mews, Pews, Brews, Stews & Dues**

Les Levine's
**CULTURE HERO**

and
Cecil King's
**Berlin Suite**

will be shown for the first time and
George Segal
will break the mould of his multiple
**GIRL ON A CHAIR**

10 00 pm 18 June 1970
RSVP
27 Kelso Place London W8

---

**Julian Trevelyan**  London Etchings

**Alistair Grant**  Azincourt Etchings

2 to 29 July 1964

Open Daily (incl Sat) 10 to 6 Thurs 10 to 1
Editions Alecto Limited The Print Centre 8 Holland Street London W8 Western 6434

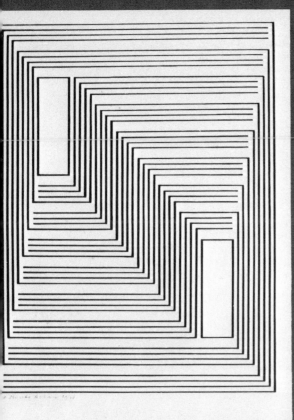

Art is not — to be looked at
art is looking — at us

What is art — to others
is not necessarily — art to me
nor — for the same reason
and vice versa

What was — art to me
or was not — some time ago
might have lost — that value
or gained it — in the meantime
and maybe — again

Thus art is not — an object
but — experience
To be able — to perceive it
we need to be — receptive

Therefore art is — there
Where art — seizes us          J.A.

18. September bis 19. Oktober 1969 tägl. 10—18 Uhr

12 Britische Artisten

Graphik
und
Objekte

Die Ausstellung wurde durch die finanzielle Unterstützung der Anglo-Elementar Versicherungs-Aktien-Gesellschaft ermöglicht.

Die Bilder dieser Ausstellung werden mit Ausnahme einiger Leihgaben liebenswürdigerweise von der Alecto Gallery, London, ausgewählt und zur Verfügung gestellt.

Künstlerhaus-Galerie
Wien 1. Karlsplatz 5

THE INSTITUTE OF DIRECTORS
ARTS ADVISORY COUNCIL
IN CONJUNCTION WITH EDITIONS ALECTO
PRESENT AN EXHIBITION OF

MODERN GRAPHICS

AT THE LONDON BUSINESS COMPLEX
BERKELEY SQUARE HOUSE
BERKELEY SQUARE LONDON W1
FROM NOVEMBER 2 UNTIL NOVEMBER 21 1964
CATALOGUE 2 6

The Directors of
Editions Alecto of America Limited

request the pleasure of your company
at the opening of the print room

1040 Madison Avenue, New York
on Tuesday, March 18, 1969

Cocktails 5:30 to 7:30 p.m.

**Editions Alecto** The Print Centre

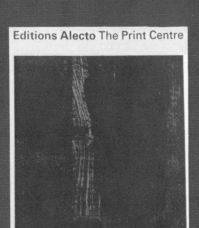

you are invited to drinks and to see two
new graphics by Jim Dine, recently printed
and published by editions alecto, titled:

Drag & WALL

and other new graphics, at Editions Alecto
Kelso Place, on Monday 14 December at 6 pm
RSVP Editions Alecto, 27 Kelso Place W.8

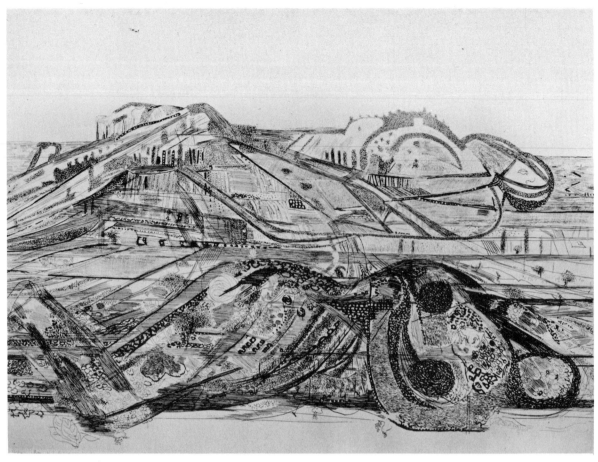

**Anthony Gross.** *Rounded Hills,* 1963. Etching, 40 x 60 cm. Edition 50.

**Alistair Grant.** *Azincourt II,* 1964. Etching on zinc, 24.7 x 32 cm. Edition 50.

Richard Hamilton. *Interior,* 1965. Screenprint, 49 x 61 cm. Edition 50.

## A DECADE OF PRINTMAKING
Charles Spencer

The origins of Editions Alecto represent that charming English genesis of amateur enthusiasm, youthful enterprise, and near-surrealist fantasy, which has produced among other things *Alice in Wonderland.*

It all started at Cambridge in 1960 when two under-graduates  Michael Deakin and Paul Cornwall-Jones were inspired, according to legend, by Julian Trevelyan's lithograph of Emmanuel College to organise prints of other Cambridge colleges.  It was but a short step of the imagination to see public schools as equally suitable or exploitable subjects. They seized on the fourth centenary of Westminster to daringly commission John Piper to make two lithographs.  Later Eton, Winchester, Downside, Charterhouse, St. Paul's, Greenwich fell into their net, the bait being artists like Richard Beer, Valerie Thornton, Ardizzone, Osbert Lancaster.  The nostal-gia and pride of the old-boys were milked, to the princely tunes of six to fifteen guineas.

By that time these two young men had transferred to Chiswick, London, where in 1962 Editions Alecto Limited was set up with the four additional directors, Anthony Longland and John Guinness, Joe Studholme, diverted from a career in merchant banking and now the only remaining founding father, and Mark Glazebrook, who later ran the Whitechapel Gallery, and once explained  'They had to make me a director because they were using my kitchen table for a boardroom '.  The history of Alecto, and indeed the total British print scene, cannot be understood without reference to the pioneering role of Robert Erskine.  Writing on the print scene in *New Society* (9. 2. 67) Benedict Nightingale noted  'most commentators date the boom as recently as 1955 when Robert Erskine opened his St. George's Gallery in Cork Street '.  Erskine commissioned, bought, exhibited, promoted the work of British artists. More importantly, as the *Arts Review* once put it, he ' encouraged the fundamental idea that one was looking primarily at printing, the imagery should come second - even a poor second '.  Annual exhib-itions of *Contemporary British Printmakers* were a feature of the gallery; the 1958 catalogue explains - ' We have chosen 40 prints by 40 artists working in British studios during the previous 12 months . . . . We have not attempted to follow any particular artistic creed, for in the graphic arts much depends on the quality of the printed image and the exploit-ation of the potentialities of printmaking . . . .'

Typical of Erskine's flair was the 25 minutes colour film *Artist's Proof* made in 1956/7 which ran four months at the Academy Cinema, London, and was subsequently screened throughout the world. (Significantly he has since become totally immersed in documentary art history for television, and film distribution).

In 1963 Alecto entered the exhibition area by creat-ing the Print Centre at Holland Street, off Church Street, Kensington.  In the summer of that year Erskine joined the board of Editions Alecto Limited and his stock formed the nucleus of the Centre's activities.

In every way this was an inspirational period in British print-making.  Chris Prater set up as an independent screen-printer in 1957, making posters for the Arts Council among others.  In 1961 he produced his first artist's print for Gordon House, which attracted the admiration of Eduardo Paolozzi and Richard Hamilton.  The latter began to interest young artists in the medium and persuaded the ICA to promote an edition of 24 prints which was completed in 1964. Although mostly young experimental artists, the participants included Victor Pasmore, whilst the influence on Kitaj and Tilson proved fundamental. These and other events resulted in Editions Alecto's desire to be involved directly in publishing, as well as in exhibiting and promoting.  In 1962 the first major work was commissioned, 16 etchings by the youthful David Hockney on the theme of *The Rake's Progress.*  When completed and exhibited at the 1963 Paris Biennale, Hockney won the major graphic award.

*The Daily Mail* of January 6, 1964, included an article - 'My Four Best Bets', in which Robert Erskine drew up investment tips in prints.  'You can still get a David Hockney for eight guineas' he wrote. Contrast that with Benedict Nightingale's note in *New Society* - 'The Rake's Progress cost 250 guineas three years ago; now it may fetch 700'.  And that was in 1967.  Ian Dunlop, writing in the magazine *Brides* in March 1972, referred to Hockney's prices as having gone up 9 times in the last five years.  Prices of all star print makers have soared, often making mockery of idealistic ambitions of a cheap art form for wider audiences.

The Print Centre in Holland Street became the principal London exhibition venue for British and foreign prints. Alongside established print-makers, such as Julian Trevelyan, Alistair Grant, Jennifer Dickson, exhibitions included artists from Hayter's Atelier 17 in Paris. Younger artists - Allen Jones, Alan Davie, Eduardo Paolozzi, Bernard Cohen, Howard Hodgkin were commissioned to produce original portfolios.

The enthusiasm of the Alecto partners expressed itself in some exciting promotions. The *British Graphic Scene* was the title of an exhibition which toured Europe in 1963. The catalogue, with a cover drawn by David Hockney, described in English, French and German, the setting up of the Holland Street headquarters as 'a determined programme of sponsorship to provide a forum for artists and a public prepared to accept the challenge and excitement of these mediums. They are, after all, the only original works of art whose price makes them available to a major section of the community'. The exhibition included works by Henry Moore, Ceri Richards, Merlyn Evans, William Scott, Hockney, Allen Jones, as well as 'craftsmen-printers', Michael Rothenstein, Anthony Gross, Agatha Sorel, Valerie Thornton and others. Later that year, November 1963, Alecto collaborated with the Institute of Directors Arts Advisory Council in an exhibition of *Modern Graphics* at the London Business Complex, Berkeley Square, London, designed to stimulate commercial patronage.

In May 1965 an even more ambitious enterprise was *Graphics in the Sixties* at R.W.S. Galleries, off Bond Street, with new works by Albers, Bernard Cohen, Alan Davie, Sam Francis, Richard Hamilton and Victor Vasarely.

By this time Editions Alecto had taken the most important step in its history, the move to 27 Kelso Place, in 1964. A former communion wine distillery, in a charming village-like street in Kensington, was magically transformed into a series of airy studio workshops for etching, lithography and screenprinting. The architect, James Madge, replaced a solid Victorian brick wall with a dashing utilitarian glass screen, and living quarters were installed to facilitate collaboration with artists from abroad.

Perhaps the two most notable visitors were the American artists Claes Oldenburg and Jim Dine; Alecto's hospitality resulted in the former's witty *London Knees* (published 1968), a mixture of graph-ics, neo-Dadaistic satire, plus a three-dimensional object; and Dine's *Tool Box,* which figured in that now famous exhibition at the lamented Robert Fraser Gallery in September 1966, closed by the police on the grounds of obscenity.

The early years at Kelso Place saw the adoption of an imaginative editorial and publishing policy, in a superb series of works and some daring experiments. Paolozzi's admiration for the skill and sensitivity of Chris Prater resulted in his famous Wittgenstein series *As is When* (published 1965), described by Ronald Alley (see page 25 ) as 'the first major statement made with screen prints'. Paolozzi established a long and productive partnership with Alecto, from which both partners have emerged with honour and international esteem. The importance of the Kelso Place set-up and the unique attitude of the Alecto partners, arose out of a mixture of the gentlemanly good-manners and respect for the artist, which marks the true amateur (in the real sense of the word), and an insistence on the most professional means of interpreting the artist's ideas and vision. Fine equipment and devoted skilled assistance were available to the artist. In the background was an editorial and publishing policy which refused to compromise on artistic or commercial grounds.

The success of the whole venture in the half decade following the move to Kelso Place is self-evident. When I chose a 10th Anniversary exhibition for the Glasgow School of Art in February 1972, I was particularly impressed by the work covering the years 1965 to 1970: Alan Davie's *Zurich Improvisations,* Robyn Denny's *Suite 66,* a series of works by Richard Hamilton including the first *Guggenheim* images, Allen Jones' *Concerning Marriages* and *New Perspective on Floors,* Patrick Procktor's *India Mother* aquatints, Ed Ruscha's organic screenprints, the *Odeon Suite* by William Scott, Richard Smith's *Triptych,* and various works by Gillian Ayres, Derek Boshier, Howard Hodgkin, Bernard Cohen and many others. The *Financial Times,* on 11 February 1967 described Editions Alecto as 'the most ambitious organisation in the field . . . . . a modern centre for the graphic arts'.

A culmination, or celebration, of this remarkable era was the extraordinary party which took place in Milan in 1968, when Alecto hired an aeroplane to transport artists and critics to attend the opening of a European sales drive at Galleria Milano. This effort inspired the *Sunday Telegraph* art critic Edwin

Mullins to award Editions Alecto his 'accolade for a display of contemporary British graphic work which made the Italian print galleries look like an ill-lit second-hand book shop' (14. 11. 68). In 1969 Alecto sent to Germany an exhibition of *12 British Artists Graphics and Objects,* with works by Gillian Ayres, Caulfield, Boshier, Bernard Cohen, Alan Davie, Denny, Hockney, Hodgkin, Allen Jones, Paolozzi, Procktor, Pye.

It is impossible to over-estimate Alecto's role as ambassador for British art. With the growing attraction of print-making to most younger avant-garde artists (a mixture of fashion, imitation, genuine desire to master technique, and a realisation of handsome financial rewards), plus the fact that the work was easy to transport and show, it became feasible to export British art on a scale hitherto unknown. The risks to all parties were low and possible returns far from negligible. Certainly in many foreign cities to which the British Council or commercial galleries would never have sent an expensive collection of current painting and sculpture, prints made known the names and styles of gifted British artists. In time this enterprise led to the large international print exhibitions now held regularly at Tokyo, Cracow,

Ljubliana and Bradford, meeting houses for the world's print output.

Alecto can claim another form of influence in the re-establishment of the old co-operative spirit, which is almost a pre-requisite for the best kind of print-making. Most continental print studios of the 19th century were really craft-workshops at which artists paid for skilled services rendered. They were rarely allowed to 'interfere' or experiment directly on the presses. You handed in your plates and you trusted on the abilities of the (often great) printers for results. Things have not changed much in France even today.

In England similar, if more limited, services existed, whilst craftsmen-printers had their own presses or used art school studios.

Kelso Place was something quite different, a freer, more informal co-operative operation, which established a pattern since repeated in the United States and other parts of the world.

The last few years of Alecto's history reflects the transitional, experimental, and to some extent, uncertain phase which art (and society) is experiencing.

**Howard Hodgkin.** *Girl on a Sofa,* 1968. Lithograph, 51 x 67 cm. Edition 75.

The purely editing and publishing basis of the operation was opened up into a direct marketing formula. Whereas formerly sales were channelled through the gallery circuit, in 1966 Alecto established its New York showroom, the same year as it opened a London gallery in Albemarle Street (which operated until 1971).

Then as a logical development from one kind of editioned art, Alecto began to be involved in the new multiple movement. There had been a number of tentative but significant steps, notably an interest in grouped images, rather than single ones, making up an artistic whole. Hockney's etchings *A Rake's Progress* are only one step away from the bound form of his illustrations for Cavafy's poems. Similarly, Paolozzi's eccentric collections of popular imagery made a more logical presentation inside a handsome plastic container. Experiments on similar lines took place with Dubuffet, Jim Dine and Anthony Deigan.

In an article for *Art and Artists,* March 1967, (long before any personal involvement) I referred to 'Alecto's heart being in creative research . . . with the prime object of searching out and examining potentially useful industrial materials and methods'.

Three-dimensionality, introduced by Claes Oldenburg's latex knees, included Peter Sedgley's motorised *Videodisques,* multiple objects by Derek Boshier and Bill Pye, Dick Smith's *Sphinxes,* the *Colour Boxes* of Robyn Denny, and Gillian Ayres' *Variants,* screenprinted enamel tiles. This period was appropriately designated *Stage 1* in an Albemarle Street exhibition in 1969. The following year David Pelham's acrylic chess set was published and saw the major undertaking of a George Segal sculpture edition.

Thus emerged the latest chapter in this history, the founding in 1971 of Alecto International. In June of that year I described it in *Studio International* as a 'logical development of Alecto's original concept (of a new social role for art) and a recognition of the urgent need for change felt throughout the art world'. This, in fact, was the beginning of my own association with an artistic enterprise long known and written about from the outside. My interest in multiplied art was the result of a growing disillusionment with the existing art situation - the over-value or importance placed on uniqueness and traditional techniques, the commercial sustenance of out-moded forms of expression, the idolatry of the art-object as investable

**Anthony Currell.** *Williamstown,* 1964. Etching, 45.7 x 30 cm. Edition 20.
**Dubuffet.** *Banque de l'Hourloupe,* 1967. Boxed set of 52 cards.Screenprint,25 x 16 x 10 cm. Edition 350.

property, the inability of traditional art to attract a popular audience. Thus, after Joe Studholme flatteringly told me at lunch that Alecto was about to incorporate some of my ideas and opinions in its future plans, I was anxious to participate in the experiment.

Like all daring and ambitious plans, it has either had to be modified or to be seen as a long-term development. It represents, however, a committment to manufactured, mass-produced art, to a distribution and marketing policy seeking a public outside the narrow, elitist gallery world, a less pretentious interpretation of the terms 'artist' and 'work of art'. As Guy Brett once wrote in *The Times*, ' With one or two exceptions multiples have remained in galleries and perpetuated the object obsession in modern art, a profusion of diverting objects rather than something that penetrates into daily life and behaviour in a new way'. All this follows attitudes which can be traced from William Morris, to Art Nouveau, to Russian Constructivism, the Bauhaus, de Stijl, and such pioneers as Duchamp, Moholy-Nagy and Vasarely.

Alecto International is now an independent company making and publishing a series of objects and prints. In collaboration with Editions Alecto they have published works by Colin Self, David Leverett, Mark Lancaster, Derek Boshier, Keith Milow as well as the first run of what I would call 'real' multiples.

The social philosophy behind the set-up echoes the words I quoted earlier from the 1963 tour catalogue - 'original works of art whose price makes them available to a major section of the community'. Thus there are ambitious and elaborate plans to take these inexpensive works of art to the largest potential audience.

Lastly there are the objectives of the Editions Alecto Collectors Club, with which I am intimately concerned. Not exactly original, since subscription schemes have long existed, but with a special Alecto flavour nonetheless. The Collectors Club is not merely a form of distribution for multiples and prints to a captive public; it will enlarge the collecting audience, and more importantly, ensure the continuance of the unique bottega at Kelso Place, where local and foreign artists can enjoy splendid and friendly facilities. Thus patronage, which in one form or another, whether state-orientated, or privately inspired, has always been essential to a lively art scene,

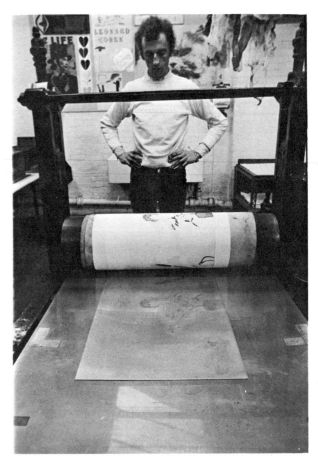

▼   The reconstructed printing studios at Kelso Place.

will be given a new, and in a sense more communal formula.

As a very recent participant in the Alecto team, I can view these past ten years with detached, critical eyes. Any shortcomings I detect seem to be integral parts of a complete conception, a basically honest and healthy realisation of the creative relationship between patron and artist, publisher or art-manufacturer and the original conception.

I have chosen this anthology as a birthday celebration. But, anxious to avoid that 'self-love' which Oscar Wilde called 'the beginning of a life-long romance', I have tried to balance 'house' documentation of some of the peak periods or major achievements with reprints of essays or commentaries from outside, on both the situation to which Alecto contributed, and the effects made by its work. Within the space at my disposal, and with as much illustrative material as was possible, I hope something resembling a fair and adequate appraisal emerges. My greatest regret is that I was unable to include a full catalogue raisonée of all Alecto publications, but I hope this worthy ambition will be fulfilled at a later date.

Finally on behalf of myself and Alecto, thanks to all those artists, authors, editors and publishers who have permitted me to reproduce written or illustrative material.

◀ **Patrick Procktor** at Kelso Place during proofing *Language of Flowers,* 1969.

**William Scott.** *Odeon Suite V,* 1967. Lithograph, 50 x 62 cm. Edition 75.

**Claes Oldenburg** becomes a London monument, 1966.

**Julian Trevelyan.** *Caius College, Cambridge,* 1964.  Lithograph, 57 x 75 cm.  Edition 70.  ▶

Artist's Proof                                                    Julian Trevelyan

**André Bicat.** *Wellington,* 1964. Etching, 57 x 55 cm. Edition 100.

◄ **Michael Rothenstein.** *Red Gothic,* 1964. Blockprint, 86 x 52 cm. Edition 35.

## ST. GEORGE'S GALLERY
Robert Erskine

**Robert Erskine** in St. George's Gallery.

St. George's Gallery Prints came about because it seemed obvious that it should. When I was up at Cambridge in the early 1950s, Heffer's Art Gallery used to hold annual shows of the prints published by the Zurich-based Guilde de la Gravure. In spite of its name, the most characteristic productions of this well-organised company were cheerful colour-lithographs by such up-and-coming Continental names as Clavé, Manessier, Singier, and Campigli; a scatter of etchings, also in colour, did justify the firm's titulature, of which the most popular were the inscrutable prints of the Chinese Zao Wou-ki. They all sold at a flat rate of three guineas, which seemed a fair enough price to pay to help a chap feel thoroughly in touch with the international swim and to annoy the hearty fellows from the Rugger Club. I bought about six, and sold them a year or two ago in Sotheby's for a 1000% profit. At the time, however, such massive returns on an unpopular investment like artists' lithographs were not to be contemplated.

The attraction of these prints for me was that they were the product of an involved technology quite unlike the straightforward processes of painting and drawing. I met a paripatetic American artist called Sam Kaner, who introduced me to the mystique of stones and copper-plates, acid and lithographic tusche, burins and dry-points and mezzotint rockers. Together we paid several visits to the Atelier Lacouriere, perched high on the Butte de Montmartre overlooking Paris, where one saluted the printers by touching elbows, their hands and forearms being permanently covered in viscous black ink. All sorts of celebrated personages flowed through the studio to admire the view, to work on a plate, or to drink the excellent Muscadet which Mme. Lacouriere kept in her Income-tax files. It was for me the navel of the world, and with the pungent odour of printing-ink hovering in the atmosphere, the foundation of St. George's Gallery Prints became inevitable.

I went around the Paris dealers buying prints for the projected shop, greenly allowing myself to be influenced in the direction of their least saleable stock: much of this impedimenta remained with me throughout the eight years that the gallery ran, ultimately to be consigned to the dustbin, rather than to Sotheby's.

No impression was to be made upon the British art-lover without an attractive leavening of famous names, so the inaugural exhibition at 7 Cork Street in 1954 contained a heady mixture of blue-chip Picassos, Rouaults, Matisses and so on. I invited my bank-manager to the opening - a bad mistake - for I remember him saying as he stared around at the exhibits "Does anybody really pay money for things like this?" Well, not many people did: printmaking was still bugged by its apparent relationship to photo-mechanical reproduction, and quite sophisticated clients couldn't bring themselves to take an art-work seriously if other identical examples existed.

However, the real purpose of the gallery was to get things moving in Britain. Rex Nankivell of the Redfern across the street had begun the good work: indeed a show of his prints by British artists had passed through Heffer's in 1952. But the energies of this excellent showman were fragmented in many other directions, and the promotion of the British print needed a full-time champion.

The first problem was to do with production and presentation. Lithos arrived in the gallery crooked on their paper, punched through with ugly registration-slots, and seldom matching the colours of the accepted proof. Etchings all too often presented an anaemic pallor where the artist had hoped for a rich velvety black. The faltering argument accounting for these horrid blemishes was that the mount would cover them up, or that people wouldn't notice: but I could only think of the stacks of superbly-printed editions on their crisp deckle-edged paper all neatly interleaved with tissue in the store at Lacouriere's. To

Helena Markson. *Queen's Dock,* 1960. Colour etching, 43 x 55 cm. Edition 100.

me, a print is a fine piece of paper with an image printed on it: it must be sold and leave the shop as such, in a cardboard roller, whatever may be the client's subsequent intentions so far as framing is concerned. So I looked for printers to professionalise the artists' output.

As the standard improved, the gallery began to have something to sell. But the customers still stayed away, apprehensive of reduplicated art. I managed to fiddle letters into *The Times* whenever the slightest opportunity arose: I mercilessly buttonholed critics and journalists and tried, without success, to infiltrate the telly. The most effective thing we did was to produce a 30-minute film called *Artists' Proof* which in straightforward documentary style showed six artists at work on the various processes of printmaking. It was obvious to anyone who saw the film

that our product had nothing whatever to do with reproductions: the artist demonstrably makes his print himself, using the chosen medium for its own sake, and not merely as a means of recapitulation to gain a wider and more plebeian market.

Many printmaking artists "belonged" to other dealers: but such was the nuisance-value of their printed work - too unpopular and too cheap to relate to the high price-per-unit customary for fully-fledged paintings - that I was always permitted to deal with them directly. Also many non-printmaking artists clearly had it in them to make very fine prints, if they could be persuaded, as they showed strong graphic potentiality in their direct work. So I bothered them, too.

Another project was to canalise the artist's print-effort into a form that could be best promoted, and

21

to do this I revived the Vollard concept of the "Suite" of prints, all deliberately derived from a single theme and published as a homogeneous series. Such were Anthony Gross's *Le Boulvé Suite* of 1956, Merlyn Evans' *Vertical Suite in Black* of 1958, Ceri Richards' *Hammerklavier Lithographs* of 1959, and many others. Habitually the artists rose to the occasion, and frequently produced their finest individual prints within the context of their suite, since the significance of a major undertaking like this provided an especial stimulus. I note with pleasure that the suite idea is still a characteristic of British publishing, very much more so than elsewhere.

Altogether, after about three years, the gallery had a good wide range to offer of respectable prints in all styles and in every current idiom, reflecting the general character of the British art scene. To make this clear, in 1957 I instituted an annual round-up of the best prints of the year, which numbered thirty-two examples crowded into the minuscule premises in Cork Street. This escalated in 1959 into *The Graven Image* exhibition which Brian Robertson generously put on for us at the Whitechapel Gallery, and our efforts began to gain attention. As a result, I managed to interest Trust Houses in the idea of using prints in their hotel bedrooms, and they undertook to finance further annual *Graven Image* shows in the big R.W.S. Galleries in Conduit Street. They offered substantial prizes for the best prints, and a talent-spotting students' section was included with more prizes donated by Guinness. Among those whom Guinness was good for in this way were the embryos of David Hockney and Allen Jones. We celebrated the first of these comprehensive exhibitions with a monster party to which the gallery invited 500 people, and Trust Houses five. The catering was organised and paid for by Trust Houses, while the capering was energised by a deafening African band. This might have undone us, I discovered later, for when I proudly escorted the dazed chairman of Trust Houses, the late Lord Crowther, around the pullulating throng, he told me, somewhat acidly, that he was also chairman of the Anti-Noise Society.

So prints and printmaking gradually entered the public consciousness, and the gallery's status burgeoned, even if its financial viability stayed where it was. Others saw that "graphics" - a nasty word like "design" - were a going concern, and I felt it was time to leave. I had at last managed to creep up the back stairs of TV, not with prints under my arm but bearing a more congenital preoccupation - antiquity.

**Graham Clarke.** *Stages at Rye,* 1969. Blockprint, 64 x 86 cm. Edition 50.

Then Alecto came along full of propagating zeal with its Cambridge Colleges and Public Schools. Rather thankfully, I handed over the mantle of St. George's Gallery Prints to them, and as a very sleepy director I now feel like an ageing uncle to a family of spirited youngsters who have grown up. Three guineas a print seems a long way off, beside Paolozzis and Jim Dines at ten times that amount, but I suppose that's what I was aiming to bring about. Anyway, it was fun and I enjoyed it. Good luck!

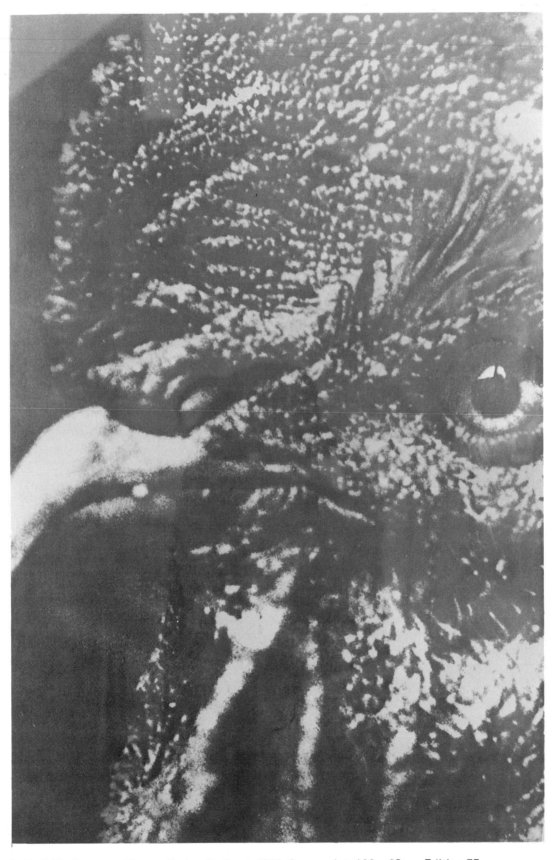

**Colin Self.** *Power and Beauty Series, Cockerel,* 1968. Screenprint, 100 x 68 cm. Edition 75.

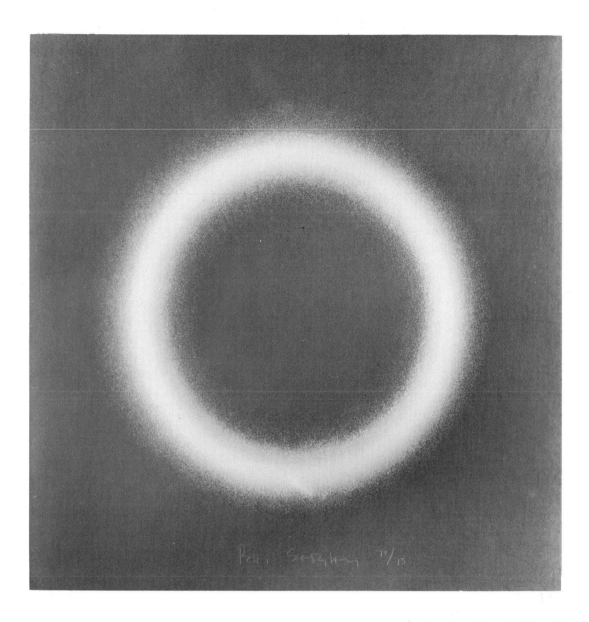

Peter Sedgley. *Looking Glass No. 2,* 1966. Screenprint, 51 x 51 cm. Edition 75.

## SCREENPRINTING IN BRITAIN
Ronald Alley

The years since 1961, when Christopher Prater made his first artist's screen print, have seen an extraordinary rise in the status of screen printing. Originally developed as a commercial process of reproduction, the screen print has come to have an artistic potential comparable to that of the old-established techniques of lithography and engraving. Although screen printing has also been used from about 1961 in the United States by such artists as Warhol and Rauschenberg, they have tended to use it in rather different, more limited ways, and the full possibilities of the medium have only been developed in England and thanks to the special abilities of Christopher Prater and his Kelpra Studio. These possibilities are ones which depend to an exceptional degree on an extremely close and sympathetic collaboration between the artist and his highly skilled technical assistants.

Looking back, we can see that the situation we have today has come about partly through a series of happy coincidences. Christopher Prater began his career as a commercial screen printer and worked for almost every screen printer in London before setting up on his own in 1957: this background gave him an extremely thorough and up-to-date knowledge of all the screen printing techniques. Then in 1958 he printed the poster for the *Young Contemporaries* exhibition which led to his printing a number of posters for the Arts Council. The transition to artists' prints was initiated by Gordon House, who is both graphic designer and painter (as a designer he has been responsible for the layout of many of the Arts Council's catalogues and posters) and who commissioned Prater in 1961 to print the series of square grids which are the earliest works in this exhibition.

The next artist to approach Prater was Eduardo Paolozzi, who asked him to make some screen prints for him. Although the earliest of these were made from collages and drawings done some years before and were purely reproductive, Paolozzi quickly began to understand that the medium had considerable possibilities of its own and started to make collages specially for this purpose, combining a wide variety of imagery and patterns and sometimes also changing the colours with each printing. He was quickly followed by his friend Richard Hamilton, who, like him, had a great interest in industrial processes and advertising techniques.

It was Hamilton who suggested to the Institute of Contemporary Arts in 1962 that they should invite a number of leading British artists to make screen prints in collaboration with Christopher Prater. Hamilton himself selected the artists, who were mostly young pop or abstract artists associated with the ICA but who also included Victor Pasmore, formerly a colleague of his on the teaching staff at King's College, Newcastle. The prints were produced in editions of 40 and were printed for the sake of economy on very thin paper. Altogether 24 artists contributed one print each, and this project, which was not completed until 1964, was therefore of crucial importance in introducing a large number of artists to the medium. Although some of them have never made another screen print since, many have gone on to produce further prints. For two of them in particular, R. B. Kitaj and Joe Tilson, the experience was a turning-point and has had a radical effect on their subsequent development: they have both devoted a substantial part of their energies to the making of screen prints ever since.

As the artistic possibilities of screen printing became more widely known, several publishers entered the field and began to commission suites of screen prints, notably Editions Alecto under the direction of Paul Cornwall-Jones and soon afterwards Marlborough Fine Art Ltd. This made it possible for Christopher Prater to give up most of his commercial work and

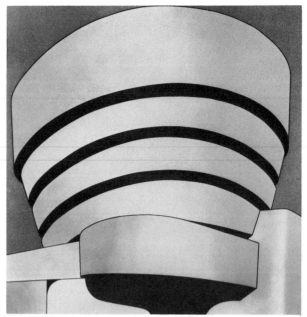

concentrate on making artists' prints. Paolozzi's Wittgenstein series *As is When,* commissioned by Alecto and published in 1965, was the first major statement made with screen prints and helped to give the Kelpra Studio the beginnings of its international reputation. Kitaj's *Mahler Suite,* sponsored by Marlborough Fine Art Ltd., was another series quickly recognised internationally as an outstanding feat of modern printmaking. With growing success and an increasing amount of work, Christopher Prater was able to move in October 1966 from the basement room in St. John's Street, which he had used for the previous three and a half years, to his present workshops in Britannia Walk and to take on a larger number of assistants. Although a crisis at Alecto in March 1967, which obliged them to cancel work on the stocks, placed the Kelpra Studio in a difficult financial position for a while, Christopher Prater managed to keep going largely through work for Marlborough Fine Art Ltd.; and before long other publishers came along, including the Petersburg Press (which had just been started by Paul Cornwall-Jones) and the Waddington Gallery. Today the position is such that he employs eighteen assistants and has so much work on hand that he is unable to to take on any further commissions for the time being. Among those who have come to work there in the last few years have been various well-known foreign artists, including the Americans Jim Dine, Larry Rivers and, very recently, Robert Motherwell.

During the 1960s there has been a widespread growth of interest in modern prints of all kinds, and the development of the Kelpra Studio and of artist's screen prints fit to some extent into this general pattern. A growing public for modern art combined with a spectacular rise in the prices of paintings has created an extensive new market for inexpensive works by leading artists.

But there were also further reasons why artists' screen prints became important at this particular period. As was stated in the catalogue when the ICA prints were first exhibited in 1964:
'The revival of screen printing of art works has been promoted by two newish developments. The first of these is the great advance made in half-tone screen printing methods by which it is possible to utilize a photographic breakdown of the image into small dots which allow gradations of tone and colour. The other is an increased preoccupation by artists with figurative, even photographic, source material. Silk-screen affords one advantage over all other printing tech-

niques - it lays down a heavier deposit of pigment. This richness of colour and body makes it eminently a painter's vehicle. Paint, and the possibility of working on a large scale without the prohibitive costs of other painting methods, have long endeared the medium to abstract artists.'

That screen printing has had special appeal for the younger generation of artists in the 1960s, that it has had greater attraction for many of them than either lithography or etching, is quite easy to understand. In the first place it is a particularly suitable medium for artists working in hard-edge colour abstract styles in that it can produce areas of colour of great saturation and brilliance. It can not only combine a large number of printings in different colours (with both strong contrasts of colour and very subtle gradations), but the colours can be varied from print to print so that no two impressions are the same. The prints by Robyn Denny, for example, have much the same subtlety and sensuous richness of colour as his paintings. The range of effects possible with screen printing can be seen by comparing Bridget Riley's two sets of prints: the first in black and white printed on perspex with clear-cut images of extraordinary concentration and brilliance, the second with very delicate modulations of greys (printed in fact with no fewer than nineteen different greys). For similar reasons it is a medium particularly well-suited to the work of Patrick Caulfield, an artist who, although figurative, works in a style very close to that of recent abstract painting, with simplified shapes and uniform areas of colour. It is therefore hardly surprising that certain foreign artists working along related lines, such as Vasarely in France and Albers in the United States, have also used screen printing with great success.

On the other hand, the technique is not nearly so suitable for the looser 'non-formal' kinds of abstract art stemming from the 1940s and 1950s which rely to a great extent on effects of brushwork and texture. This helps to explain why it has been comparatively little used by the more senior British artists.

But above all screen printing seems to meet the needs of certain artists associated with pop art, such as Richard Hamilton, Eduardo Paolozzi, R. B. Kitaj and Joe Tilson, all of whom are interested in a deliberate interplay of styles and in photographs, films and advertising techniques. Much of the originality of Kitaj's early paintings executed before he started to make screen prints lies in the way a number of con-

◄ **Richard Hamilton.** *Guggenheim,* 1965. Screenprint, 57 x 55.8 cm. Edition 50.

**Robyn Denny.** *Suite 66,* number three, 1966. Screenprint, 76 x 51 cm. Edition 75.

trasting elements, some of them figurative and some abstract, are fused together. This is an approach which he has been able to develop yet further in his screen prints, working not from a preliminary collage but from a selection of photographs, patterns, pages from books, drawings and so forth which he arranges and modifies as he goes along. The prints are the result of an extremely close collaboration with the cameraman and other technical assistants on whose skill and patience he makes enormous demands. And while Kitaj pushes the medium as far as it can go in one direction (one of his prints *Die Gute Alte Zeit* required no fewer than eighty-one workings), it is Joe Tilson who is constantly experimenting with screen printing on moulded plastic and other unconventional materials, and with attaching a wide variety of appendages to his works.

Another artist unconnected with pop art who has made use of the photographic basis of screen printing to achieve effects which cannot be obtained with any other print medium is Harold Cohen. In his suite of prints based on a photograph of Richard Hamilton, the breakdown of the image into dots is used to create a series of almost completely abstract colour patterns.

In selecting this exhibition from over six hundred artists' prints produced by Kelpra Studio, the main emphasis has been placed on those which make full use of the screen print medium instead of using it simply as a means of reproduction. As will be seen, it is a flexible medium which allows a wide range of treatments. This exhibition celebrates a remarkable new development in British art.

*This introduction to the catalogue to the exhibition* Kelpra Prints, *held at the Hayward Gallery, London, 17 June to 17 July 1970, is reprinted by permission of the author and the Arts Council of Great Britain.*

Patrick Caulfield. *Coloured Still Life,* 1967. Screenprint, 56 x 91 cm. Edition 75.

## ALAN DAVIE'S ZURICH IMPROVISATIONS
Paul Cornwall-Jones

At the lithography studios of Matthieu in Zurich, the craftsmen are absorbed day to day in printing weather charts for the Swiss Government. Now and then a painter arrives, hiding himself in a small cubicle adjoining the main press area, appearing occasionally to supervise the proof taking from the plates on which he is working. In general, the atmosphere is slow, almost indifferent; tucked away in the corner a massive Neapolitan steadily grinds used stones to recreate the sensitive surface from which a fresh image by another hand will soon be taken. There are racks and racks of stones, set on end with small identification numerals stamped or stuck on the rough edged cross-grain: occasionally a scrawled name hints of other possibilities: 'Marino' on this, 'Francis' stamped heavily on a mammoth double elephant block six inches deep of heavy Bavarian limestone. There are five flat-bed presses on this floor, presided over by the Master Printer, Monsieur Chere, and manned by German or Italian assistants. Monsieur Matthieu himself organises and delegates the daily programme, hurrying between his craftsmen, and huge elegant self-inking flat-beds on the solid concrete below. These are the long run presses, that print colour over large areas without a ripple or blemish.

One feels here a wealth of technical knowledge and a set pattern of activity. The accepted methods of making artists' lithographs are dominated by the innovations of Picasso and the atelier of Paris in the thirties, fourties, and early fifties. In general these men co-operate with their artists, but still maintain a critical reserve that leaves some void in the act of making. One felt this strongly on Alan Davie's arrival; this new face would soon be schooled into a well worn pattern, with little upset in the daily routine. He would disappear for a day at a time into his small cubicle, producing maybe a deeply chalked stone for their expert hands. It was his speed and activity that first caught them by surprise.

Language difficulties were swept aside as he moved from one press to the next, delighted with the qualities of superimposed inks impossible to obtain by other methods. The craftsmen were puzzled, as forced to quicken their pace, plate upon plate appeared followed by Davie with instructions to print in varying order and colour; there began to develop images with two, three, or four printings and involved composition. For all their techniques, he wanted the medium used his way with his rhythm; quite slowly they warmed to this approach as various combinations were tried, resulting in the preliminary series *Ghost of a Chance* . The plates for the *Zurich Improvisations* were started the next morning. The initial intention was to make three separate images with five plates each, but as the proof taking continued, Davie began to mix the first colours and then the plates themselves, achieving a fantastic web of startling proofs that spread around the studios, as assistants moved frantically to turn his programmes into fact. Through the day the atmosphere grew sharper, and by evening exploded as it dawned on these men that for once, perhaps for the first time ever, they were in on the act, an integral part of the operation, not only technical observers, but definitely relied on to react intuitively to each different situation. From that moment there was no holding them; indeed, this communal excitement led to their own improvisations which were presented proudly for inspection - so much so that the artist found it difficult to keep up with their growing enthusiasm. The colours glowed amidst the tangled knots of line, and purely lithographic possibilities are accentuated where flat black on black on black achieves something quite different from other three dimensional mediums. The excitement of the event shows strongly and one can only welcome such an uncompromising stimulant for others to experiment in these fields.

*Reprinted from catalogue for the exhibition at Gimpel Fils Gallery, London May 1965.*

**Alan Davie.** Two images from the suite *Zurich Improvisations,* 1965, a portfolio of 34 prints. Lithographs, 63 x 90 cm. *Improvisation XX* edition 25, *Improvisation I* edition 75.

**WILD TRACK FOR LUDWIG** The Kakafon
Kakkoon laka oon Elektrik Lafs
Eduardo Paolozzi

The first of the four labyrinths, stagy, divided as it
is into long dialogue scenes formally framed by a
limited number of establishing shots, yet the teacher
steps aside of the doors, the battens being held in
position by four screw eyes, as used in most theatres
for a like purpose, or stout and strong gimlets would
answer, dwarfing such objects as naturally develop
to a great size, but are likewise fond of unnaturally
developing objects which in a wild state are insignif-
icant. Aeroplanes, Horse-races, Boat races and the
like, have a certain popular value Mechanised
melody Melodious interpretation of mechanical
theme . . . consistently medium tempo. The continuous melody is on strings and brass with french
horn predominant, supported by staccato wood wind
and muted brass phrases. Definite ending. The
buildings leaving behind only stones and bits of
rubble and he replies "What we are destroying is
nothing but houses of cards and we are clearing up
the ground of language on which they stand". Juxtapositions, they would find out the connections between the two pictures for themselves. They would
guess what the pictures meant to say. They would be
the artists whose imagination observe the Laocoon
group with care. To my surprise I have found several
crucial restorations that have significantly changed
the composition of the group but have not been taken
into account in its recent reconstructions. The
correction of these faults might choose for example,
not the white or the black box but the box which
was to the right or left, in accordance with its experience in the previous test. This would be the
wheels which were of brass and had eight spokes,
give the meaning but destroy the picture. The sense
is here, however, nothing; the picture everything.
Juxtapositions had been born. The plane is nearing
the target. From the inner-phones comes the pilot's
warning; "Pilot to bombardier - On course and
flying level". As now placed, the sun seems fixed by
the coils and base that join him and his father in a
relief; hour on hour they kept up this busy whirl,

stopping for neither meat nor drink, until finally the
Bedouin's horses would drop in their tracks, and
the riders would fall from their saddles, panting and
exhausted. He began to give instructions, although
there were times when he felt he had dried up. He
wrote a rather dull paper for the Aristotelian society
but when the meeting was held, he talked of something different. Point of the composition, which in
its main lines is carried up and back, like a great
wave by the twisting movement of the central figure
and the complementary forms of the flanking sons.
That only the first test of the memory series would
be of value as an indication of the existence of a
previously acquired habit. Even under the conditions
of no shock and no stop nothing is too great, nothing
too trivial to ask; the heavens must respond with the
blows of his hammer, and his left hand must indeed
relax its hold of his sack-mouth if all petitions are
granted on that day. A dull thunder, a rolling sound,
from the height surrounding Rizza . . . it was the
sound of the guns, of the wagons, of the footsteps
that pulled ever towards thin wooden rods, then
wound round the rods. The length of the threads
must allow the actress to cross the stage and disappear
into the side wings in which the action was unified
in a comparatively shallow space. All this nonsense
may thrill the misinformed multitudes, but its use-
fulness ends right there. For the flight testing of
aircraft is a careful, studied science almost totally
without heroics of the Hollywood variety. Two
wooden partitions which are pivoted on their main
vertical axes so that they could be placed in either of
the positions indicated how the deepest emotion
produced by the first could prejudice the one that
follows. Any want of effect in the second must be
owing to its inherent want of pathos. A cord A.
In the diagram a forest scene is being changed into a
cottage interior the bottom of the scene that moves
across the stage has a few domes of silence hammered
in. The sun sank with its burning arrows. The
soldiers marched, bowed and grim. The air boiled
thickly and threatened to choke them. The hills on
the left held their breath. A solitary cloud on the
horizon. Dull clothes being blown about. The actress leaning forward as though struggling against the
wind, as she walks away from the manipulator of

the threads. A scene of inevitable destruction. The younger son, helpless, his legs bound, his body crumpling, lapses into unconsciousness and death, fatally wounded. The band played while members of the engineering department brought out ropes and pullies, cables and derricks, beams. The general public knows little of him. But he has a softer side. He has written a poem, its last lines run "did you hear what the bird said?" "I did" said Algebra "it is made in small pieces". That a man has been taught the ordinary use of words "the same" in the cases cases of "the same shape", "the same length" give point to his argument, the Grand Master then conducted his audience to another part of the forest. Can the dancer learn a regular labyrinth path more quickly than an irregular one? Now to the left, now to the right running in circles, passing through it would eliminate the extraordinary cleavage of directtions. Pictorial figures may be substituted for circles. Safeguarding the operation of these elevators free flowing scrawl work designs of a floral character. Stage effects sound heavy of beams falling, which sound may be got by a muffled big drum or a heavy piece of wood, as a post is held vertically and brought down with a thud upon the stage. The band, palm up in a gesture eloquent of horror and futility, like the forearm was bent backward and down, in the direction of various sound effects required from time to time as birds singing, a policeman's or railway quard's whistle, ducks quacking, a fog horn for a ship at sea and other semi-musical instruments, all of which suffer from no lack of systematic books. No nation in the world surpasses us in the faculty of deducing from a couple of definitions and tremble at the idea of soon seeing Medea in her unmitigated ferocity, our imagination far outstripping the slightest attempt at symmetrical arrangement; indeed, any thing like uniformity or balance of parts appears to be studiously avoided in these groupings. Wind is graphically expressed, birds are perched cleanly cut and perforate patterns the trees waving in the summer breeze, in Autumn stripping blasts, and with barren branches weighed down with winter snows; firmly anchored to the wrist, by its constricting motion the reptile also pulls the lower arm down, lifting the elbow and severely averting butterflies, and symbols of various kinds. As a distant castle suddenly becoming ruins or disappearing altogether and a forest taking its place, or it may be an interior scene with bare walls, when instantly three houses collapsed to be called out to prevent any explosions size, imagination can hear him cry, if he cry imagination can neither mount a step higher, not fall a step lower without seeing him and certain elements acquire new meaning intensely baroque in nature. The younger son's death becomes a surprise, the head of the snake, that point which leaves the observer to imagine the crises without actually showing it, and in uniting with this not so essentially transitory as to become offensive when the first company had returned. How miserable the poor devils looked with their faces pale as ashes, with weary deep-sunk eyes, he like a plane

**Eduardo Paolozzi.** Six images from the series *As Is When,* interpretations of Ludwig Wittgenstein, 1965. Screenprints, 96.5 x 65.4 cm. Edition 65.

*Wittgenstein the Soldier.*          *Wittgenstein in New York.*          *Artificial Sun.*

of action common to the three figures. There is, however, no continuous connection fixing this position. But his home was in Berlin, and when he laughed he opened a tremendous mouth, the simple opening of the mouth apart from the violent and repulsive contortions it causes in the other parts of the face, is a blot on a painting. The six wise men marched on as steadily as they could, for not only was the ground shaking under their feet, their knees were shaking too. They marched right out to Algebra's front door, opened it cautiously and went in. Then they got into the elevator and pushed the very top button. The assistant who manipulates the thread held a rod in each hand, giving them a see-saw motion, raising and lowering them and now and again giving them a slight pull. The above movements and others brought about by practice will serve to unify the two figures forcefully. The son's raised arm and his slightly inclined torso nicely complement the adjacent masses of the father's figure, while the raised legs are repeated motifs, wires of the interrupted circuit, it receives a shock as a result of the closing of the key in the circuit by the experiments by means of the handle. This allows snow to gradually escape through the slots. It, the snow storm, is a prolonged one, a second assistant supplies more snow-flakes. There are some more practical aspects which conjecture is free to play upon. One lies in powers mode of understanding the world. So far Plato's problems are continuous with the modern philosophers; but they are discontinuous too in so

far as neither poetry nor religion nor science not mathematics not metaphysics is now tubing, and forming, cupping, or bending sheet. The material hardens as it is worked, but the operations are seldom severe his love for irregularity gets its full scope in the disposition of his varied devices, the more we must think we see. But no moment in the whole course of an action is so disadvantageous in this respect as that of its culmination. Sky blue; white clouds; foliage green; poppies brown with black caps. Cut ovals adding triangular caps after. Clouds, free-cutting, but a few curved lines placed far above the tops of mountains or tall growing trees; when low and rain charged, they are disposed in horizontal masses across the outline of a mountain. Mist is depicted somewhat in the manner of Zipatone eccentric using Xylophone, Tymps, Piano. Mysterioso, with Tymps and Tambourine. He heeled down and got into a vertical dive. He was almost four hundred yards behind the bomber when he opened fire. He saw pieces of fabric disintegrate, saw the bomber weave fantastically and then a plume of black smoke issued from the starboard engine. Tympani roll, with Cymbal in unison. Rhythmic Tymps with Tambourine background. He did not paint Medea at the moment of her actually murdering her children but just before. What he thinks and knows. How to find fictional correlatives for his beliefs. The result is so violent as to extort a scream, either soon abates or it must destroy the sufferer. *Original text for the* As Is When *folio, 1965.*

*Reality.*

*The Spirit of the Snake.*

*Wittgenstein at the Cinema admires Betty Grable.*

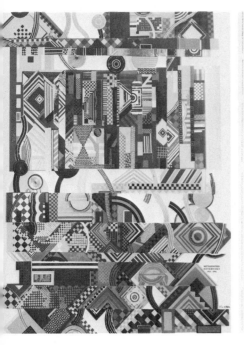
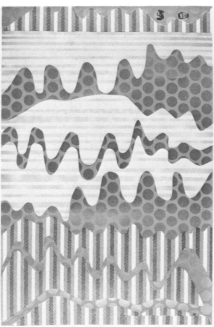
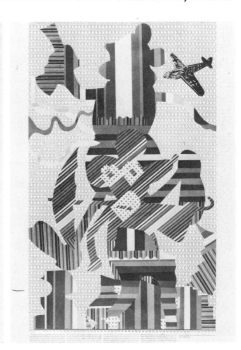

Eduardo Paolozzi. Poster for *As Is When,* 1965.

Eduardo Paolozzi. *Parrot* from *As Is When,* 1965. Screenprint, 80 x 55 cm. ▶

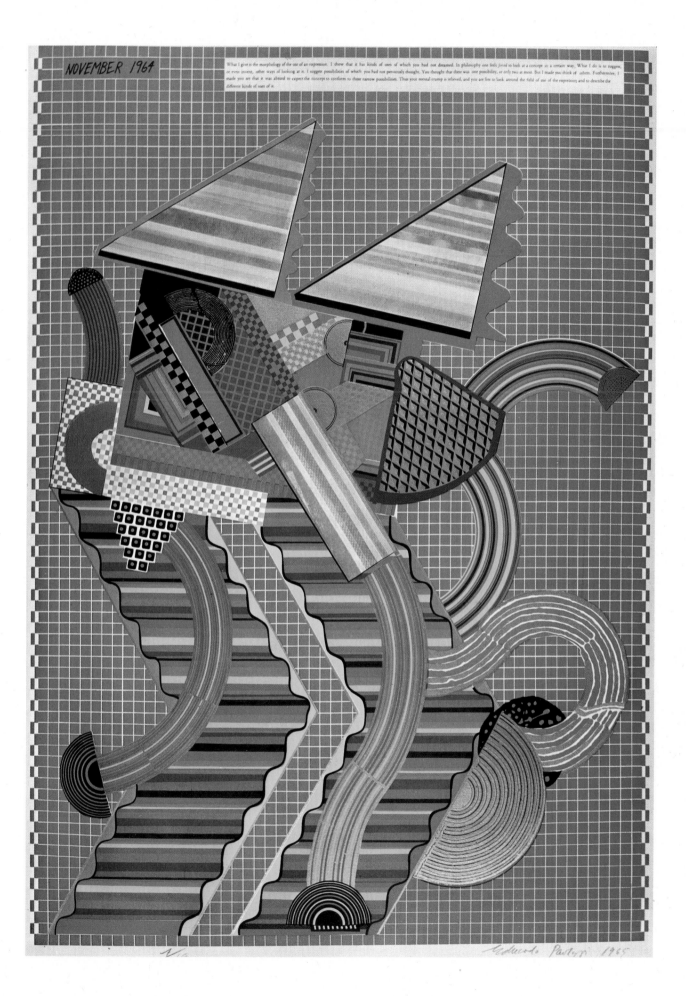

NOVEMBER 1964

What I give is the morphology of the use of an expression. I show that it has kinds of uses of which you had not dreamed. In philosophy one feels forced to look at a concept in a certain way. What I do is to suggest, or even invent, other ways of looking at it. I suggest possibilities of which you had not previously thought. You thought that there was one possibility, or only two at most. But I made you think of others. Furthermore, I made you see that it was absurd to expect the concept to conform to those narrow possibilities. Thus your mental cramp is relieved, and you are free to look around the field of use of the expression and to describe the different kinds of uses of it.

**Allen Jones.** *Hermaphrodite Head,* 1964.  Lithograph, 76 x 56 cm.  Edition 75.

◀ **Allen Jones.** *Icarus,* 1968. Lithograph, 69.7 x 101.6 cm. Edition 75.

# A LICENCE TO PRINT ORIGINALS
Benedict Nightingale

As 1966 drew to its dismal end harassed capitalists threw aside their investment portfolios, looked up at the walls around them and felt comforted. It was the year of Rembrandt rather than Rootes, Braque rather than BMC. True, the best speculation was nickel: it rose in value by 135 per cent during 1966. But after that (according to *Pick's World Currency Report)* the wise investor put his faith and wealth into works of art. Apart from op, pop and American non-objective, everything did well: "old masters" improved by 15 per cent, tapestries by about 50 per cent, sculpture by 60, and, best of all, original prints, lithographs and posters, by 70 to 80 per cent.

Last year Sotheby's broke two records for print prices. Rembrandt's etching *The Three Crosses,* went for £30,000; *The Women's Bath,* an engraving by the mysterious 15th century artist known as "the Master PM " for £32,000. Lithographs by French impressionists, often selling for sums well into the thousands, were at least four times as valuable as they were ten years ago: "We have difficulty finding enough to satisfy the demand for them,"says Adrian Eeles, the firm's leading print specialist. Indeed, the signs are that the value of all original prints, Durer to Blake to Renoir to David Hockney, is continuing to rise sharply. Hockney's 16-print series, *A Rake's Progress,* cost 250 guineas three years ago; now it may fetch 700. Prints by William Scott which sold for 15 guineas four years ago now sell for 40 or 50; prints by Allen Jones which cost only 12 guineas three years ago have been sold for 100. These artists have become increasingly fashionable during the period; but the longer established have also appreciated in price. A litho of Henry Moore's *Seventeen Reclining Figures* cost 40 guineas in 1964; now it fetches at least 100.

As the demand for prints grows and prices rise, so the publishers flourish. Most commentators date the beginning of the boom as recently as 1955, when Robert Erskine opened his St. George's Gallery in Cork Street. Paul Nash, Edward Bawden, Graham Sutherland and others had, it's true, done posters for Shell and London Transport in the thirties; but their example, and even that of Picasso, busy with lithographs abroad, seems to have had little impact on British artists in general. Erskine pointed out the possibilities of the medium, commissioned prints and put on an annual exhibition devoted to them, *The Graven Image.*

Soon afterwards the publishers moved formidably in. Curwen Press started its lithographic studio in 1959: it has published prints by Moore, Scott, John Piper, Ceri Richards, Alan Davie, and others. Editions Alecto started quietly in 1960. Michael Deakin and Paul Cornwall-Jones, both in their early twenties, managed to convince Westminster School that it wanted a couple of lithographs in honour of its 400th anniversary, and then persuaded Piper to execute them. Two years later the partnership became a company, and, in 1963, published Hockney's *A Rake's Progress:* · its first substantial success. Recently it has commissioned work from Barbara Hepworth, Alan Davie, Eduardo Paolozzi, Allen Jones, Bernard Cohen, Victor Vasarely, Jim Dine: it has a New York office and a growing export business.

Marlborough Fine Arts, too, may sell as much as half an edition in the United States. It started its print department in 1964, and has many of the most prestigious artists under contract: Piper, Pasmore, Nolan, Moore, Ceri Richards, and others. Every November it holds an exhibition of 60 different original prints, specially commissioned from its artists. Marlborough is cagey about its finances; but it seems safe to declare it the richest, easily so, of the three.

Marlborough and Alecto publish only in limited editions: Alecto up to 150 copies, Marlborough 75 or less. Any edition of more than 75 is regarded by the authorities as a commodity rather than a work of art and becomes subject to purchase tax,and, if it is being imported from abroad, duty. One of the odder responsibilities of Marlborough's prints manager, John Martyn is to go to a building near Middlesex Hospital, open those packets of lithos his firm has had printed abroad and number his edition in the presence of a customs officer. All limited editions, lithos or screenprints, must not only be carefully numbered, but also individually signed by the artist: collectors insist on evidence of his participation in the preparation of the print and of his approval of the finished product. Signed prints by Picasso may fetch as much as 375 guineas, unsigned ones as little as 18.

\* \* \* \* \* \* \*

Value, clearly, has no necessary connection with the aesthetic calibre of an offering. Indeed, the com-

**Allen Jones** signing prints at Kelso Place.

Colin Self. *Power and Beauty Series (Car),* 1968. Etching, 68 x 100 cm. Edition 75.

mitted print collector resembles nothing more closely than the collector of first editions who won't cut the pages and read the text for fear of sullying an *objet d'art* and damaging an investment. For instance: if it is invisibly glued to cardboard, if the white surround is cut to fit an aesthetically suitable frame or a ragged edge trimmed, if it is *anything* but clipped virgin to a backboard, a print will certainly lose much of its value. It may no longer be readily negotiable currency.

This is the point. Purchase tax may encourage a publisher to limit an edition to 75 rather than to 100; but it can't by itself explain an overwhelming bias in the trade. Why limit editions at all? The practice has the sanction of tradition. Collectors, apparently, like to luxuriate in the feeling of enjoying something only a very few other people can enjoy. "A person who's paid £72 for a Sutherland likes to think that there's only 75 copies, and that his is the ninth of them," says Martyn. "He doesn't want to think that there's 5,555 others going around too." And then the market for modern lithos and screenprints is very limited: the public at large still prefers to buy its art at Boots." If we printed more copies, we could reduce the price," says Felicity Schwartz, Alecto's office manager, "but I still doubt if we could find as many as 2,000 people to buy them." A certain amount of money has to be raised, to cover royalties and other costs. When the artist is prestigious, the amount will be large. The limited

edition is a way of making a virtue of the inevitably of small sales, and hence of justifying economic prices. Besides (the apologists go on) would it do an artist any good at all to glut the galleries with endless copies of the same print? Better, surely, to keep the turnover faster, the artist consistently occupied with saleable new work, the public's interest whetted by continually changing images.

It may be true. But the fundamental reason for limiting editions is quite other: it is economic in a different and (for many) depressing sense. If a collector buys the seventieth copy of an unlimited edition, which so far amounts to 1,000, it is likely to appreciate in value much, much slower than the seventieth copy of 75. Indeed, if the edition doesn't eventually sell all its 1,000 copies (and, since the market *is* limited, this could very well be the case) it may never appreciate at all. If it does sell out, then the publisher may keep prices down by running off another few hundred copies. "If there was only one of that, it would cost you £900." says Martyn, pointing at a £50 lithograph by Oskar Kokoschka hanging outside his office. "And then, we could make it an edition of 7,000, and sell them for ten bob each. But, if we did that, you wouldn't be selling your copy at Sotheby's in ten years' time." The limited edition, he thinks, is a happy medium between total exclusiveness and total licence.

A rigorously enforced medium, one might add, at least when a reputable publisher like Marlborough is involved. There is no danger of reprinting on the sly. The zinc plate, or stone whatever is used, is ritually defaced when the required number of copies has been run off: an extra copy is then run off to prove that this act of scrupulous vandalism has indeed taken place. Occasionally—and, it seems, mainly abroad—a printer may sell the plate unharmed, and extra copies appear on the black market. Forged Blakes have been in circulation for years: nine out of ten copies of some of his best-known engravings are said to be phoney. But now the forgers are turning their attention to modern artists: only the other day, says John Martyn, someone came into Marlborough with what looked like an original Jackson Pollock—and wasn't.

There are, too, those who still believe that the quality of a print must deteriorate after a certain number of copies have been run off: among them, David Sylvester, who wrote in the *Sunday Times* recently that it was "technically impossible to achieve over a long

printing run the sort of richness and density of colour and texture which can be got over a short run." This isn't an opinion shared by the printers and lithographers themselves. Christopher Prater (who does screenprints for Marlborough and Alecto), Stanley Jones (manager of Curwen's lithographic studio) and both of them idolised by publishers, artists and dealers, see no impenetrable technical barriers. Modern processes can, it seems, preserve plates almost indefinitely. Eric Ayers, one of Alecto's directors, talks in terms of a quarter of a million copies. Stone —that is, limestone, mined in Bavaria—may deteriorate unless sympathetically nurtured; but it, too, may

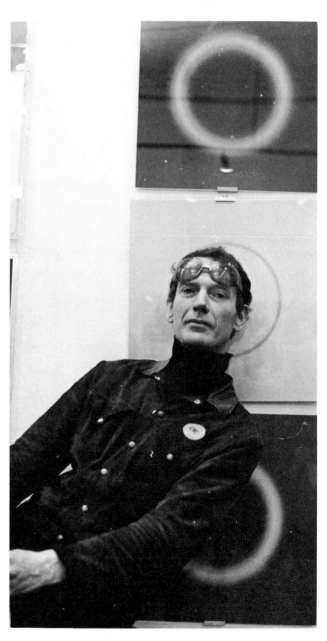

Peter Sedgley with three images from his *Looking Glass Suite* of nine screenprints,1966. 51 x 51 cm.Edition 75

be good for an edition running into many thousands. This presupposes immense care with inking and colouring: it is best to have the artist as well as the master printer, continually on hand. In practice, it's true, the artist doesn't always see the run through to the end. When it is to be a long one, he simply signs a proof copy (a rarity, incidentally, highly prized by collectors) and leaves the printer to simulate it. But there seems no reason why this should *necessarily* be the case; no reason why he shouldn't be persuaded to stay longer; no reason why the ten thousandth copy shouldn't be as good as the first one.

\*    \*    \*    \*    \*    \*

Unfortunately, the distinction between "works of art" and "commodities" isn't confined to the inland revenue. Publishers seem quietly convinced that the ten thousandth copy must somehow be less "original" than the first—in spite of the obvious fact that they both share an identical source, the plate or stone on which the artist actually worked. If the first copy can be rated a work of art, then so must the ten thousandth, provided it comes up to technical scratch: if the ten thousandth copy is a mere commodity, then so, necessarily, is the first. However, one classifies the them (and it is, perhaps, only a matter of a convenient label) they are both, to an equal extent, reproductions.

Yet, of the three main publishers, only Curwen brings out "original" prints in unlimited editions: about 60 fo them so far, priced at 52s. 6d. a copy. The artists (including Geoffrey Ireland, Richard Bawden, John Piper, David Gentleman) tend to be more conventional than those in limited editions; but it is something that they are freely and cheaply avail-able at all. Again, the other publishers tend to insist that sets of, say, six or twelve prints should be purchased as a whole; Curwen believes in breaking them up and letting those who want individual prints have them. Elisabeth Frink's *Spinning Man* series, eight lithographs in all, costs 165 guineas, but its individual components may be bought for as little as 20 guineas each. "We don't believe in selling in sets", says a Curwen executive. "The only customers who can afford them are institutions or rich collectors. We don't believe in high prices at all. Our basic philosophy is that original prints should be available to quite ordinary people."

It all depends on how one defines "quite ordinary people." The other galleries would say that quite ordinary people nowadays can afford, say, poorish Rembrandt prints at £30 or £40, if not poorish Durers at £150 to £200: and Philip Sutton at 12 guineas, Bernard Cohen at 18, Richard Hamilton at 30, if not the whole Eduardo Paolozzi set *As Is When* at 500. The average price for original lithographs and screenprints still seems to be under 20 guineas.

Little enough, one might think, compared with the price of anything decent in oils; but, given the technical possibilities, the expertise of men like Prater and Jones, given that the barrier to longer runs and less limited editions, is, in the last resort, the collectors determination to plaster their walls with a decorative equivalent of stocks and shares— is it little enough?

*Reprinted from* New Society *9 February 1967, by permission.*

**Bernard Cohen.** *Lithograph I,* 1966. Lithograph, 55.8 x 76 cm. Edition 75.

**Allen Jones.** *Third Bus* from the portfolio of five prints
*Fleet of Buses,* 1967. Lithograph, 63.5 x 55.8 cm. Edition 20.

**Allen Jones.** Poster for *Life Class*, 1968. Offset lithography,
85 x 55 cm. Unlimited edition.

**Mark Lancaster.** *Eight Colours* from *Henry VI Lithographs,* 1971.  Lithograph, 60 x 78 cm.  Edition 30.

**Derek Boshier.** *PLAN 1,* 1972.  Offset lithography.  Edition 100. Alecto International.

# A TOOL BOX
## by Jim Dine

screen printed and assembled by
Christopher Prater at Kelpra Studios LTD.
in april 1966 London, on various
materials and papers chosen by the artist
and the printer. Each print is 19" X 24".

Published by EDITIONS ALECTO as
Portfolios of ten images in numbered
and signed editions limited to 150
with 30 sets of artists' proofs.

Jim Dine, London
april 1966

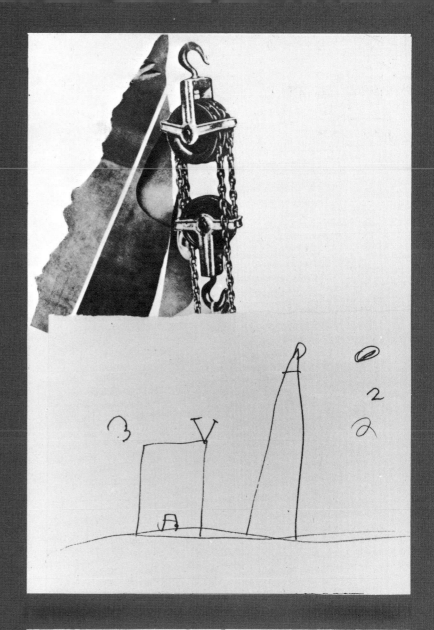

**Jim Dine.** Two images from *Tool Box,* 1966, a portfolio of ten prints. Screenprint and collage, 61 x 49 cm. Edition 150.

**Jim Dine.** Image from *Tool Box,* 1966, a portfolio of ten prints, 61 x 49 cm.

Screenprint and collage. Edition 150.

# JIM DINE'S TOOL BOX
Cyril Barrett

In his last exhibition in London (at the Robert Fraser Gallery last year) Jim Dine paid tribute to Mary Quant and other aspects of the London scene. (That was before *Time* had discovered 'Swinging London'.) But at that time Dine had not yet visited London. Since then he has been working here and has produced several series of collages (*London, Thorpe-le-Soken, Dine-Paolozzi)* a series of gouaches *(Lips)* collage prints *(The Tool Box)* and blown-up photographs.

What is surprising about this work is that, though it was done in London, and one of the series bears the title *London,* it makes no direct reference to London. It is an indirect tribute. 'I did them there in London', he says, 'because it is what it is, because to me it was privacy and respect for it. I experienced a kind of new freedom there, formally and emotionally.'

Dine found that he was able to do things in London which he would not dare to do in America. For one thing, he could trust his judgement. The blown-up photographs, which he did in collaboration with Michael Cooper, are the result of nothing more than straight choices of what he and Cooper considered visually interesting. Personal choices of this kind would not, he feels, be respected in America.

London also gave him a different attitude towards America. It taught him to accept certain aspects of American culture—industrial design, for example— which most Americans would not regard as cultural. 'We're still so young and naive culturally that one thinks of art as a very high thing.' It took people like Richard Hamilton and Eduardo Paolozzi (and not, incidentally, the strictly 'pop' painters) to bring this home to him. In the *Tool Box,* which is the first series of collage prints of its kind (and a credit to the printing skill of Editions Alecto), he incorporates screen prints from industrial design magazines and old-fashioned engineering textbooks, as well as pieces of plastic or metal, into his very elegant compositions.

Dine also experienced a certain ambiguity in London's respect for personal freedom and privacy. This is reflected in the series of graffiti called *London* and in the collages made from material supplied by Paolozzi (the *Dine-Paolozzi* series). The English respect for personal freedom, while it shows a certain delicacy and refinement, springs partly from a reluctance to get involved in other people's idiosyncrasies, problems and enthusiasms, and from a refusal to face any fact which may be unpleasant or embarrasing. At all costs one must maintain the fiction that everything is sweetness and light. Everything is wrapped in roses with a Selfridge's wrapper. But this is not so much respect for freedom as a cold, rather impersonal tolerance of it.

Dine, on the other hand, is warm, spontaneous and straight. In his *London* and *Dine-Paolozzi* series he attempts to dispel some of this reticence and sweetness by a bald statement of fact: This is how things are. We are all human under our genteel wrapper.

One has to acknowledge Jim Dine's sincerity in making these works. They are not in the least lascivious, pornographic or erotic. Scatological, they may be, but there is no hint of a snigger. They are perfectly in line with Dine's other work in which he takes ordinary objects (a suit, a saw, a washbasin) and presents it, divorced from its ordinary functions and surroundings, as something to be regarded dispassionately for its own sake. In this case he has taken the solitary scribblings of frustrated men or rebellious adolescents and in a sense redeemed them by endowing them with style and a gentle humour. Such is the temper of the times, however, that it is not unlikely that they will be treated with a solemnity which they hardly deserve, and Dine's name linked with that of Genet, Miller, Burroughs and Kenneth Tynan. They are, after all, little more than a mild protest, a gesture of independence; once again it's the "sailor on leave" and it's the child's first time away from home, that sort of thing. Besides, they are not so very revolutionary; Duchamp and the Dadaists made the same point a long time ago. They may cause embarrassment to some. If so, it will be on account of their sincerity as much as anything else. A respect for privacy may reasonably be expected to work both ways, and the Englishman who is reluctant to wear his heart on his sleeve may quite naturally resent being forced by others to look at theirs.

*Reprinted from* Studio International *September 1966, by permission.*

**Gillian Ayres.** *Lorenzo the Magnificent and Niccolo the Gear,* 1967. Screenprint, 78 x 58 cm. Edition 75.

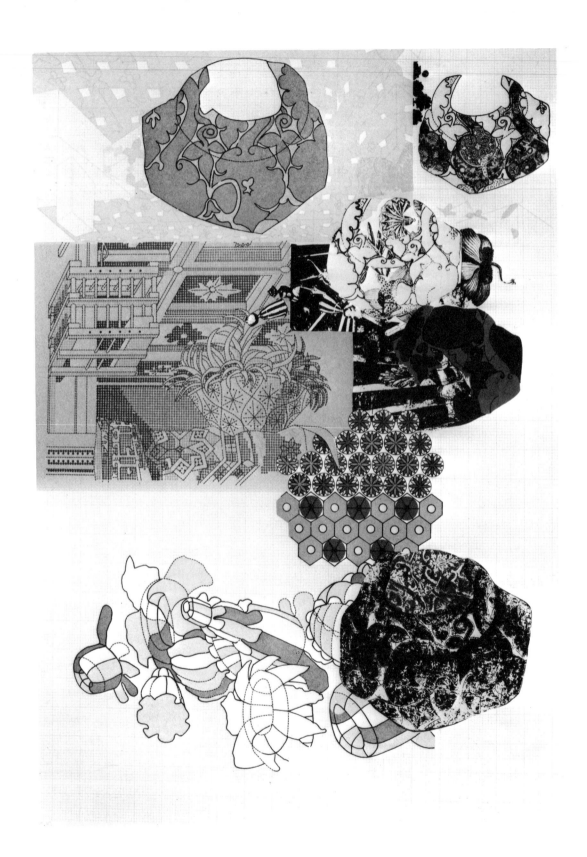

## THE NEW GENERATION: OPPORTUNITIES AND PITFALLS
Bryan Robertson

A new generation of young painters and sculptors is rapidly asserting itself to a remarkable degree. Its sheer talent is self-evident, and this is reinforced by an uninhibited flair for self-projection. A fortunate swing of the official and commercial pendulums towards active support of the young is also in its favour. There was a time when only more obviously tried and seasoned talents could gain recognition or even a hearing. It now remains to be seen whether private and public patronage in this country will rise to what amounts to an unprecedented situation.

It is not enough for these young gladiators to win prizes and prestige abroad, or for the public at home to sense the sharp attention suddenly paid to our young artists by foreign critics and dealers. English private collectors, and, above all, the English corporations and commercial houses should realize the urgency of retaining a sense of their own contemporary culture and of backing it in the most practical manner. If this does not happen, the depressing flight of gifted young scientists across the Atlantic may well be followed by a similar migration of young artists in search of more enlightened and more generous patronage in the United States. A considerable proportion of the elements which nourish both their visual consciousness and even their thinking already flow, abundantly, from America—a sad reflection on the decline of popular culture in England during the past decade.

The mental climate in this country, however, or, more practically, actual working conditions, are as pliable and undemanding as an old glove; and this subtle comfort of intercourse, travel, communication, and the ability to be at peace in a studio, may well hold our artists back. Many American artists, weary of the excessive chauvinism, the lack of intelligent yardsticks, and the hothouse jungle of the New York scene, have sensed the liberal, friendly breadth of the working atmosphere of London. Certainly the new fusion of the two sides of the western world, America and Europe, is nowhere better demonstrated in recent years than in the give and take between London and New York which has taken place in the visual arts.

There is much to be said in favour of this new generation of artists in England, and what must be said so positively does much to characterize the actual nature of its gifts. A complete and very healthy break with tradition, for instance, involving a total disregard for precedents or, more particularly, any noticeable sense of the way an English artist is supposed to paint, let alone the subject of his painting. It is felt, clearly, that enough has been said about landscape, for the time being. If anything is said about the human condition, then it will be within an urban environment and there will be alienation devices in the handling, for a common characteristic of this generation is an all-pervading coolness of tone and manner.

**David Hockney** working on his *Hollywood* series.

If the work is completely abstract, then an abstraction is made which is barer, more completely self-sufficient, than preceding examples. Most of these artists, whether abstract or figurative, share an almost obsessive distaste for the rendering of space in depth. There must be no recession. The flatness of the picture plane must be respected: space can thrust forwards, three dimensionally; or even sideways, thus disrupting the conventional vertical or horizontal boundaries of a canvas—but space must never, never, recede.

There is much else to observe, but of crucial importance is the new element of absolute professionalism to be found in this new generation. Their paintings and sculpture are impeccably made while disdaining the old principles of fine craftsmanship *per se,* or truth to materials as a noble objective in its own right. The new professionalism has taken in its stride an equally new arrogance towards technique and materials: everything is pressed into service if it serves the image. This professional confidence, so precociously deployed, is not, however, without its hazards: an over cool, thin, English, well-tailored look about the cut of certain paintings and sculptures of the past two or three seasons has struck a warning note.

A more subtle source of danger resides in the actual usage of talent: what you do with your talent once you have it. Here, there sometimes seems to be a hostile force in English society itself, intent upon emasculating talent or making it more acceptable in an enfeebled sense, and which seeks to undermine

this same talent by a warm display of encouragement and applause. Wyndham Lewis, though not without traces of paranoia, was conscious of this force in England.

An artist whose created image seems diminished, at this moment, from a purist's viewpoint, might well be Mr. Sidney Nolan. The strength of his variable but often magical talent has suffered from over-exposure. For if you are Leonardo himself and you produce, hypothetically, Leonardo greetings cards, and illustrate articles in newspapers with Leonardo drawings, and design a ballet, and travel down the Nile for a magazine and thus produce Leonardo sketches, and hold an exhibition of paintings at one gallery and a show of drawings at another while, at the same time, Leonardo dust jackets are banked in tiers in booksellers all over the country—and appear in person in a Leonardo film on television—then, suddenly, the public will become weary and your image, over-disseminated and over-worked, will seem lacking in surprise or, more seriously, any real meaning.

And so Mr. David Hockney's double exhibition of *The Rake's Progress* prints (at the Print Centre, Holland Street) and paintings (at the Kasmin Gallery, New Bond Street) gives one pause for disquieting thoughts. At the preview party for the prints show, for instance, Mr. Hockney's prints were around the walls, Mr. Hockney and his friends were among the guests, and on a blank wall at one end of the gallery a television screen projected the additional image of Mr. Hockney being interviewed on a

**David Hockney** *Figure in Front of a Curtain,* 1964. Lithograph with screenprint, 48 x 60.8 cm. Edition 75.

**David Hockney.** Three images from the set of sixteen prints *A Rake's Progress,* 1963. Etching and aquatint, 30 x 42 cm. Edition 50.

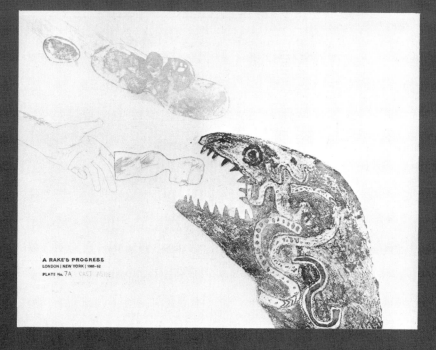

51

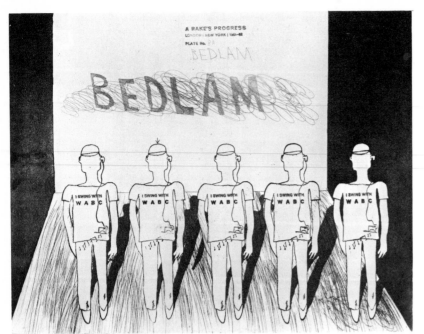

**David Hockney.** *Picture of a Still Life which has an Elaborate Silver Frame* from the suite of six prints *A Hollywood Collection,* 1965. 76 x 57 cm. Edition 85. ►

**David Hockney.** Image from *A Rake's Progress, 1963.*

popular television programme. Meanwhile, Mr. Hockney has also been sent down the Nile by a well-known newspaper in exchange for drawings, and has produced a cover—a disquietingly indifferent one—for a magazine and there have been other eruptions on the scene, including a public self-analysis at the I.C.A.

Now, quite clearly, artists do not have to suffer the tedium of the ivory tower if they prefer the hurly burly of the market place. And, equally clearly, all artists at heart believe—sometimes with alarming reason—that they could easily keep at bay the combined machinations of General Motors and all the newspaper editors in London, let alone their dealers. But the game is not worth the candle, for however they may delude themselves to the contrary, it is the artists who are continually exploited and usually wrecked, through loss of time and vulgarization of their image. And Mr.Hockney's image is, in fact, thin and sharp, but also delicate. He should conserve his strength for his work.

The sequence of prints, happily, is a total success: edgy placing of images, a fastidiously dry sense of the juxtaposition of black and white and a highly individual formal sense, wiry but not untender, drive home at a spanking pace the up-to-date whimsically autobiographical version of the *Rake's Progress* morality tale, based here on the artist's own escapades in America. The final print of robot-like figures with their transistor sets, rendered in a deliberately mechanical line, brings the series to a sardonic conclusion. In the paintings, however, the very virtues of Mr. Hockney's graphic work seem to weaken his executive powers as a painter. For what

appears to be eloquent and beautiful as pure white space on paper seems empty and unfulfilled on canvas and the very wit and delicacy of his sophisticately naive figures in the drawings becomes, too often, merely pawky in terms of paint.

Mr. Hockney seems to have a rather cold and unsensual gaze on the human figure, tinged by a curiously middle-aged, sentimental regard for some aspects of his personages. Too often, the resourceful sense of graphic lay-out does not entirely compensate for a lack of real structure or composition. The colour, similarly, goes through the motions of brightness, but it is cold, northern, and entirely joyless and unsensual. In both the drawings and the paintings, the use of words and letters seems an unnecessary concession to a revived fashion and does not add anything to the composition—except, perhaps, to keep any traces of reality at bay. Alienation rears its head again.

It remains to be said, however, that the show of paintings, with its perspective dodges and its curiously artful artlessness, is an extremely personal accomplishment. Perhaps a more direct concern for real life, rather than photographic substitutes for life, might provide a parallel means for a greater depth and breadth of vision. Meanwhile, this talent should be tenderly developed and not cast to the four winds of exploitation.

*This article first appeared in* The Times *(London) on 17 December 1963 and is reproduced by permission of the newspaper.*

52

◄ Group of sculptures in George Segal's New York studio including *Girl on a Chair*.

◄ **George Segal** in his New York studio with the original sculpture for *Girl on a Chair*. (Photo: Hans Namuth)

## GIRL ON A CHAIR

R.B. When I was last out at your house, George, I saw many fragments of a body strewn on the floor of your studio - that is , plaster casts of various aspects of the female body we so naturally favour. Would you feel back into the relationship of these fragments to the boxes you're working on now?

G.S. The fragments must have begun from some kind of erotic or sensual impulse, to define bits of lips, fingers, breasts, folds of flesh, intricate lines. Usually, I put the pieces together to make a complete figure.

R.B. Will the fragments remain independent or will they find themselves as elements of larger works? They keep lying around in my mind. I like them as they are.

G.S. Probably stay as themselves, as independent thoughts or sensations. They provoked a lot of questions for me: they looked beautiful strewn around on the floor or when I picked them up and handled them and looked at them casually and intimately. What were they: notations? loving comments? lyric statements? glimpses? If I left them on the floor, they were like leaves. If I put them on the wall, they could be a bit out of a Cubist collage. I remember some Cubist paintings as bits and pieces of the real world strewn on a canvas to make a musical harmony. My memory of walking down a city street has to do with the glimpses of things I've seen that stick in my mind. What's composition? Maybe it's walking along and encountering my own glimpses. What's the edge of a glimpse? We see 180 degrees wide but can focus on a small detail, only dimly aware of the rest of the field. With a camera we can choose arbitrary limits as a metaphor for psychological focus. Couldn't I carve out an arbitrary chunk of space and see a glimpse of a figure in relation to part of an object in relation to that amount of space? That thinking provoked the *Girl in the Chair* in the black box. It also provoked this wall of boxes which is a metaphor for walking down the street and seeing glimpses of different things. I'd like to turn a corner and feel a wrenching shift of scale, like being high in the air and looking down at the city at night . . . . . . I'm working on that.

R.B. Did you conceive *Girl on a Chair* as a multiple?

G.S. No . . . . that piece was one of a series of fragments and boxes on which I had been working. When the opportunity arose with Editions Alecto to make a multiple of anything I wished that would satisfy me aesthetically, the *Girl on a Chair* seemed right. I accept plaster as a final material. Traditionally, it's used to make moulds for reproduction, and is discarded in the transition from clay to bronze. The wooden chair was originally mass produced, and I had made the box using standard lumber. It seemed natural to use those same materials.

R.B. You seem very comfortable and clear in this box. Certain pastels of yours come immediately to mind: one group, of a half dozen or so, of the model in a chair from your 1964 exhibition that I thought of as strongly architectural. This box has fewer elements in it than the other two boxes I saw and seems very tangible, more direct, like the pastels. Were the pastels a source for the box?

G.S. Yes . . . . I've made a lot of pastels using that chair. That same chair has been knocking around in my studio for years with the funny steps cut into the back of it. After having been drawn so often, it's finally been incorporated into a sculpture. The chair is like a ladder with steps the box is like a house, the girl is like a Greek caryatid holding up the roof . . . . . I've always liked the hardness and softness combined, this wedding of organic and geometric.

R.B. In the behind where it meets the chair, it doesn't flatten out, like she does in real life.

G.S. I picked the fragments up from the floor, sat it on the chair in the box, didn't have the heart to smash those two perfect curves with a hammer, and figured, well, it could be just the moment before contact . . .

*Original text issued on the publication of George Segal's multiple* Girl on a Chair, *1970. 91 x 61 x 38. Edition 150.*

Pages from *Fourteen Poems* by C. P. Cavafy, 1966. Illustrated by **David Hockney** and translated by Stephen Spender and Nikos Stangos. Reproduced by permission of Mrs. Kyveli Singopoulos and The Hogarth Press.

## Caesarion

Partly to inform myself about a period,
partly to pass away the time,
last night I picked up a collection
of inscriptions of the Ptolemys to read.
The same abundant flatteries and adulation
are lavished on them all. They are all brilliant,
glorious, powerful, benevolent;
all of their enterprises are very wise.
As for the women of the family, they too,
all the Berenices and the Cleopatras are marvellous.

Having informed myself about the period
I would have put the book aside
had I not chanced upon the name
— in a brief reference — of king Caesarion . . .

Ah, there, you come with your vague charm.
There are only a few lines in history about you,
and so I was the freer to invent you in my mind.
I made you handsome, sentimental.
My art adds to your face
a dream-like sympathetic beauty.
And I imagined you so fully
that late last night, as my lamp was going out —
I let it purposely go out —
I thought you came into my room,
it seemed to me you stood before me; as you would be
in conquered Alexandria,
pale and exhausted, ideal in your sorrow,
still hoping to be pitied
by all those wicked people — whispering "Too many Caesars".

C.P. CAVAFY IN ALEXANDRIA

A.P.                                             David Hockney  66

Double, revolving clippers of the "Philishave".
All deuce objects: Scissors, Plugs, Lightswitches, Biplanes.
See the bland Knees, like pudding, in the "How to Draw" book.
Rembrandt's Susannah (?).
They suggested Johns' beer cans.
Telephone receiver – Knees.
One could tell time by the Colossal Knees.


Knees in space, to be turned in space. Never look "right". Hands itch always to adjust them. Must be grasped to move them. (Therefore, "kinetic".) Knees moved by hands.


Portland Place called a Knee joint.
A light inside a taxi in the form of a back of a Knee.
An obsession here in London with the Up and Down – influence of the tide.
Feeling up London.   London "feels".
Should the Victoria Embankment Knees move?  Various positions – striding for example, or waiting for a bus.


I spend most of my days standing. Knockknees like mine make good architecture.
Knee equals Gear Shift.  Riding for a long time in a small English car one feels the bent Knees.
The Colossal Gear Shift proposed as alternative to the Trafalgar monument moves at five minute intervals, flipping from one position into another suddenly and shaking the sidewalks.

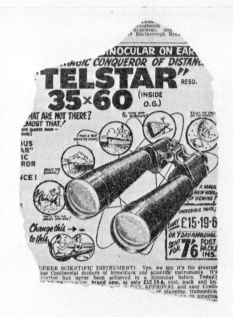

BINOCS

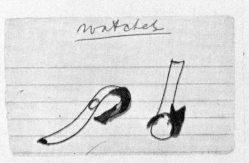

watches

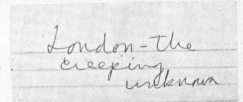

London - the
creeping
unknown

C066

Fat Back-of-the-Knee Monument.
I started with the backs of the Knees because that is what one mostly sees,
Knees ahead of one, walking at the same pace, or walking away.
The child's head is at the level of the Mother's knees.


The plain objects must link up with cultural landmarks.
Baden-Powell monument – his naked Boy Scout Knees.
Waitresses Knees – enlarge through use of calipers.
1066–1666–1966.
The tubes *are* tubelike.
How utilize the Thames reflections on my ceiling?
Fraser knocks the silver off the table.
Faucets equal Knees.


At art school, the Knee was the most difficult part to draw.


If the Knees are used as Lamp Bases, a warm light falls around the Knees
from above.
Lampettes – Knees.
Salt-shakers – Knees.
Chealsknee.
Knees – Fireplace Logs. Module of Fireplace-Knees for the Official
Charnelhouse of Pornography.
Knee – Toilet Bowl.
Knees – Flexible and doublebarrelled Ray Guns.

London 1966

Knees = to Toilet.

FIRES
WITHOUT
HEAT

SNACKS

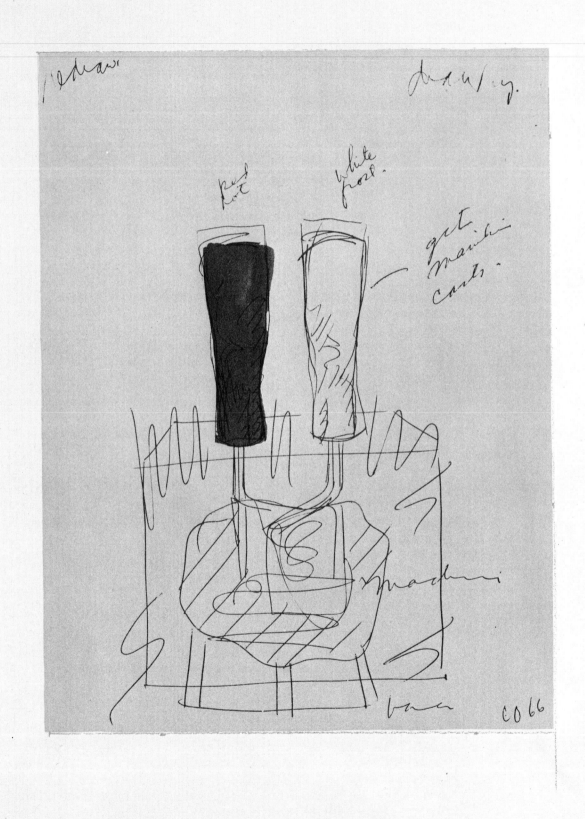

*"Hot and Cold Knees"*

The multiple *London Knees, 1966* was published in 1968. Cast latex, 35 cm. high. Edition 120.

## ROBYN DENNY'S COLOUR BOXES
Robert Kudielka

Robyn Denny's work is unmistakable. In all its permutations the quality of the colour remains constant; the various forms retain a common image; the colour is flat tone. The tonal quality does not refer to solid colour values; it is not a departure however, but the same principle, applied to the scale of the spectrum. Colour *is* quality. The form is determined by the 'entry image'. The formal construction follows in stages starting from the lower edge of the picture; the lower centre of the picture therefore appears as the threshold, through which the spectator enters. The entry-image and tonal colouring are the immediate characteristics of Robyn Denny's work.

His series *Colour Box* still keeps to the specific quality of tone in his colour. But the colour values are no longer restricted to the range of grey, green, blue and brown: the darker mixtures are replaced by clearer colours. In this series the colours of the objects are combined to form a circular composition; the colour used for the entry image appears in the next object as the basic colour. With a boldness unknown until now, Denny introduces a brilliant orange, or the blue/yellow contrast. This does not mean that the principle that the quality of colour precedes its physical value, is abandoned; on the contrary, the further Denny penetrates into the spectrum, the more clearly the qualitative interpretation of the colour emerges. The colour in this new work cannot be ascertained immediately as 'red colour', 'green colour' etc. The eye is too preoccupied with the constitution of the tonal light objectively to register the colour at once. The reality of the surface pigments becomes obvious only when the viewer realizes how decidedly this colour resists arbitrary moods.

The formal changes/innovations in the series *Colour Box* are more far-reaching than the change in the size of colour. Above all, the reduction of the vertical vectors, which Denny has been pursuing for some time, has never reached the point it has now in the present work. The format and the forms appear to be more relaxed than before even though they more and more approach the square. The vertical symmetrical axis however remains unchanged; it is even more accentuated by the colour. In consequence of the emphasis on symmetry the entry image comes more to the foreground. Entry image and symmetry are used to complement each other in Denny's work: the tendency to draw the viewer into the picture is compensated for by the hermetic structure. In the series *Colour Box* the counter-weight of the symmetry is of particular significance as the entry image is emphasized here by a new composition principle. The layers of planes of clear acrylic allow the entry of the view not to appear as a mere metaphor: the eye wanders indeed through various stages into the picture.

But not only is Denny's treatment of form clarified and made more precise by the layer principle; both characteristics of his colour come out more sharply-colour as pigment and colour as quality. The concrete form of the appearance of colour - its material and physical presence - is clarified by the diverse levels of the planes. Difference in colour is also difference in mass. On the other hand, the immediate sensation of colour gains in intensity: the depth of tonal quality of shade loses the semblance of mere illusion and becomes through the stacking in space a real event.

Precisely, the precision of the colour elements favours 'a more ambiguous interplay', as Denny himself says.

Finally, the stacking principle allows the parallel between use of colour and the formal elements to become clear. The structure of these multiples is hierarchical and rectangular, its colour matte and even; structure and colour are on the surface. The other aspect of Denny's work is based on the fact that immediate discovery accompanies objective contemplation, and this sees the structure as architecture, the colour rich and deep; architecture and tonality constitute the picture. The unity of form and colour within these categories is a basic principle of Robyn Denny's work. But never before did he separate out his components so analytically as in the objects of the *Colour Box.*

The unity of picture components corresponds to the unity of impact. The artificiality of the separation between 'immediate' and 'objective' reveals itself in the ambivalence which characterizes the elements of viewing. In *Colour Box I* for instance the eye moves immediately into the picture when it keeps to the two violet steps of the entry image. (Denny suggests the picture be hung only a few inches off the floor.) The three red areas which are graduated from the front towards the centre, represent the objective unity of the work; their concentric structure hinders the penetration of the eye. The relation, however, becomes the exact opposite when the viewer starts from the perimeter edge (contours?) of the picture. The sequence of the three red areas causes an immediate concentration on the focal point of the picture, because the relation of the picture to the proportions of the human figure does not permit a renewed confrontation. The two violet right angles, the corner stones of the entry image, now appear as a disturbing obstruction: they establish the distance of the object. The ambiguity of the picture phenomenon reveals the ambiguity of the onlooker's position: he is in front of the picture as well as in it, he is participant and viewer at the same time. The presence of Denny's work is determined by the co-presence of the viewer.

The *Colour Boxes* only become objects of confrontation when one 'enters' them. Experience and awareness of experience constitute a peculiar unity which appears to fall into the phenomenal-logical category of 'appresentation'. This conception however is misleading if it is understood in its usual context; because it signifies, generally speaking, the power of reflection, something to visualize, which one notes immediately. In contrast the relation in Denny's pictures is basically reversed: they are objects which force the viewer into spontaneous activity. The picture is an invitation to become productive in its frame; the work itself appresents the viewer, not the other way round. For Denny the autonomy of art means not only that the picture is independent of the existence of the viewer. He understands by autonomy that the work itself is the reason for the effect it has - the participation of the viewer.

The *Colour Box* series shows again that Robyn Denny's art is to a large extent classical art. There is no need for reference on the part of the viewer to relate the picture to one's own experience of the world; that by-passes the essence of Denny's art. The relationship to the picture is determined not by the viewer, only by the work itself. The natural tendency to relate oneself to things in the world is suspended; the participation of the viewer excludes his taking other things into consideration. In this sense the horizon of the picture opens before the viewer. He remains in the picture, even when he tries to make it an object.

The viewer experiences through the phenomenon of the horizon what 'world' means: one is part of it, no matter how much one may try to visualize it as an object of awareness. In daily life the world is usually obscured by the things in it. Robyn Denny's work, however, makes 'world' manifest in almost absolute purity in as much as all relations to things in it are barred. Denny's art does not make things visible, but man seeing.

Reprinted from *Studio International* January 1969 by permission.

**Robyn Denny.** *Colour Box, 1969.* Screenprinted acrylic sheets, 61 x 50.8 x 5 cm.

**Richard Beer.** *Christ Church, Newgate* from the portfolio *Ten Wren Churches* with a text by **John Betjeman,** 1970. Etching and screen process, 77 x 55 cm. Edition 75.

# CHRIST CHURCH, NEWGATE STREET
John Betjeman

This is the saddest of the ruined churches in the City. One reason is historical, the other architectural. The mediaeval Franciscan Friary Church which stood here was even longer and broader than King's College Chapel, Cambridge. The nave and choir, as at King's were separated by a screen. It was a place of Royal sepulture and contained the heart of poor Edward II and the body of Isabella his faithless Queen. In fact the Friary Church, with its many marbled tombs, tiled floors and marble columns, must have been a rival to the Cathedral of St. Paul, nearby. At the dissolution of the monasteries the Friary Buildings and library were turned into a school for poor boys, known as Christ's Hospital-the Blue-coat School. After the fire of 1666, Wren and his assistants rebuilt the Grammar School and in the 1820s, John Shaw the able architect of St. Dunstan's-in-the-West, built the Infirmary, the west side of the quadrangle and Great Hall in a correct late Perpendicular style. There may still be Londoners alive who remember the old Christ's Hospital Buildings, which stood where now the General Post Office's Edwardian extension and noisy yard right up against St. Bartholomew's Hospital. The school was removed to Horsham in 1902 and London saw Bluecoat boys no more, except when they came up once a year to the Spital Sermon in Christ Church. Lamb and Coleridge were educated in the London buildings, and in the church near the pulpit, the Reverend James Boyer, was buried, of whom Coleridge remarked "It was lucky the cherubim who took him to Heaven were nothing but faces and wings, or he would infallibly have flogged them by the way".

Wren rebuilt the church after the fire on the foundations of the eastern end of the choir of the old one. Wren's church consisted of nave and aisles of seven bays, with a western tower with three entrances to it, and a fourth opening into the church. It was an enormous preaching hall, a forest of dark woodwork with tier galleries rising round three sides. In these galleries until 1902 sat the Bluecoat boys in semi-darkness, for most of the daylight was admitted through clerestories in the vaulted ceiling of the nave. This vaulted nave ceiling had bands of decorative plaster and was supported on Corinthian columns, panelled up to gallery height. There was much fine woodwork on the twin pulpits and in the large western organ case. Best of all was the east end, with its Commandments boards and plaster scroll-work and Royal Arms, above the east window. I remember the church well of a Sunday evening, for I enjoyed the preaching of its rather Evangelical incumbent, Prebendary Hine-Haycock-the ticking gallery clock, the smell of polished wood, the sense of ghosts of listening hundreds in the galleries. Incidentally the device of using galleries in tier in aisled churches and round three sides, much pleased Wren, and was copied in most churches throughout the 18th century. Since 1940 the scene of all that sculpture and oratory has become waste ground, wired in, continually broken into, and littered with tokens of modern pleasure, newspapers, cigarette packets and broken plastic, through which weeds try to sprout. Up on the east wall are the scorched remains of plasterwork. The ruins are on a key site in a greedy age. But there is something uncannily strong about its history and atmosphere which still keeps it (1970) open to the sky.

The one benefit that Christ Church has received since the war is the restoration of its steeple by the late Lord Mottistone. The steeple was built, as was so often the case, some time after the body of the church. It was not completed until 1704. It is a square contrast to the curve of St. Paul's dome. The Youngs, as usual, describe it well. "Very tall, precise, rather aggressive, rising in variagated squares." Before the war the spire looked as though there was something missing from it, and it was not until Lord Mottistone placed the twelve urns back on the parapet over the square Ionic temple halfway up the steeple, that the whole design regained the perfection it has today. Unfortunately the steeple cannot now be seen in relation to St. Paul's as its designer intended us to see it. The slabs which the Church Commissioners built on the north side of St. Paul's, cut it remorselessly across, where they do not obscure it altogether.

*One of the essays written for Richard Beer's portfolio* Ten Wren Churches *published 1970.*

EXTRACTS FROM INDIA MOTHER. AN UN-
PUBLISHED DIARY, JANUARY/MARCH 1969
Patrick Procktor

**Jan 8**

. . . . . coincidences are the real excitement; as a
'plane finally appeared when depressed passengers
felt it never would, the sky suddenly opened into a
fantastic vault of transparent sapphire indescribably
rich and varied with imperceptible transitions into a
rose horizon, the scale open to one's eyes dwarfing
the trifling solitary Trident on the tarmac.

**Jan 9**

What are those common little birds, a half inch
taller than a sparrow, with dramatic black heads
cresting almost at a right angle and circular white
patches at the side? The body is a soft grey with
slightly brown wing feathers. Beak is short. Every-
body knows except for me. Basrah is full of birds.
The trees between the landing strip and airport building last night were full of birds singing for all their
might, a better form of greeting to the illiterate than
the arabic sign reading welcome. At the Raghdan
Palace Hotel (more like a garage) a pathetic little
tree outside my window was full of song this morning.

**Jan 10**

Strange troubled dreams. With polished toecaps I
am stepping along a muddy street with thick rich
lustrous ridges of sand, and honeycombs of mud-
puddles. Ahead a huge puddle has grown into a lake
filling the width of the street, the water is jade green,

impassable, fathomless, there is a little reddish light
in the deepest part (like the blind eye of my mother's
pekinese).

**Jan 12**

. . . . . I left and walked to the river embankment, a
really beautiful sight, the first vivid colours of sea,
distant palmgrove on the opposite shore, painted
wooden boat moored a few yards in front of me with
dusky sailors loading and unloading dates. I quickly
went back for watercolours and hastily sketched. It
seemed as if the sun went down between one brush
stroke and the next. One moment the palms were
bathed in a golden sunset so that I could not see
what was pink and what was green, and the next I
looked up, the trees were dark, the water turned
paler than the sky which it reflected. Then night,
giant stars and a crescent moon.

**Jan 16**

. . . . . I work too much. Sometimes I'm too ingrat-
iating. I picked up my sketch from the chair on
deck and showed it to the Bringer of Light from
Yorkshire to the State of Kuwait and his broad.
'Very nice.' Then the daughter churlishly 'Got 'ny
more?' I go on, turn the pages, show three or four
'I like the sunrise' says mother. 'Looks as if it needs
finishing' corrected the surly girl. End of scene in
30 secs flat. Much better if I had not offered.

Jan 23
Opal light as we arrive. Daffodil moon still high at day-light. Below the moon the windows of houses on the shore reflect the sun in topaz gleams.

Jan 26
Malabar dawn - delphinium blue shadow of myself against a wall in the hanging garden. My two little old men cleaning the room as I write.

There is some secret in that blue surrounded with white-pink golden light close to painting (pure colour shapes on a single plane), beyond painting. I am sure that the surface is not really flat, the single plane is not single but a microcosm of all planes, infinite to mind as soon as we open our eyes.

Feb 2
In the morning I walked round the lake, starting in a clockwise direction from the nadir of dejection, expecting to meet a diamond-headed snake or at least a scorpion under every stone. By degrees the bird-song, the distant music of children, and women carrying stones, the little goatherd and his tall and gentle goats, a pale girl in a Volkswagen, green corn-fields below me as I strolled along the parapet of the lake, the simple exuberance of nature rescued my spirits and restored my balance.

Feb 8

First attempt with pure 1920 hand-made Indian paper.

*Peculiar* paper: drinks water the tooth takes the colour at the first stroke and leaves the water on the brush. But it *also* takes large clear colour!

And a straight contour!!

Feb 10
My imagination just refuses the perfection of the Jain carvings and architecture; but the tinkling bells, and six hundred years old mango trees in the temple, and to see Frank pick a leaf from this long-living thing and put it in his pocket, later to cure the tinnaca on his ankle, these I appreciate.

March 7
In the golden evening we strolled into a field. I turned my back to the light and started to paint green and gold dabs of the flowers and corn before my eyes. More children came. Hallam hated my picture. More children came, watched me, left me to watch my friend. One little girl stayed alone by me. By good luck as light faded we caught the bus and bumped, on the crowded back seat, our way to Kathmandu.

*Patrick Procktor's* India Mother, *a suite of seven aquatints was published in 1970.*

**Patrick Procktor.** *Rowli Mountains* from *India Mother,* 1970. Aquatint, 43 x 61 cm. Edition 60.

**Patrick Procktor.** Two images from the suite of aquatints *Invitation to the Voyage* 1969, *Sadie and Prudence,* 25 x 45 cm., *The Language of Flowers,* 45 x 75 cm. Edition 75. ▶

B A T, Dav                                    Petrid Pallya

**Edward Ruscha** with ingredients for his organic screenprints.

◄   **Edward Ruscha** at Covent Garden selecting materials for his organic screenprints *News, Mews, Pews, Brews, Stews and Dues,* 1970.   58 x 81 cm.   Edition 125.   (Photo: Tony Evans)

# TALKING TO ED RUSCHA
Christopher Fox

Edward Ruscha is an artist from Los Angeles of growing interest and reputation. Last year's exhibition
of Pop Art—at the Hayward Gallery—included a representative selection of his works. Recently, at Editions
Alecto, he has been working on a project by the use
of the silk-screen process. Or, rather, by a personal
and inventive employment of that process of printmaking: foodstuffs, crushed flowers, syrups, and
sauces have been used in the place of the conventional
inks. The artist has turned, so to speak, the laws of
printmaking to the advantage of his explorative imagination. Much of his earlier paintings were distinctly
marked by suggestive allusions or direct reference to
food. Indeed, the print was often intended to give
an image of sensuousness calligraphically; the most
obvious were like icing on a cake. Behind the lettering
would be a colour bearing a continuous or complementary tonal relationship to it. The degree of syn-
chronization between word and meaning, colour and
texture engendered, because of their plastic isolation,
further connections with the environment from which
they were drawn. They were humorous.

We are forced to see the new prints through a reverse
channel: the earlier work was read in terms of the
degree to which the image assumed an illusionistic
sensuousness; in the present work we have to view
sensuousness as an image. There is a reversal of
tendency.

I talked to Ruscha about his present project and,
more generally, about his view of himself as an artist.

'Right now, I am out to explore the medium. It's a
playground or a beach, so I'm going to send as much
sand up in the air as I can! I think the next time I'll
print with iodine.

I have to be in control of the medium. The organic
elements have to combine satisfactorily. What I'm
interested in is the possible range; also in the use of
a *processed* media.' Ruscha does not narrowly con-
trive the possible effects of his project: rather, he
wishes to cut to a minimum the number of possible
accidents. It is the control in the unpredictable area
which he enjoys. But control for him does not mean
rigidly transposing a preconceived image in print; the
latitude for chance 'goes hand in hand with it'. Yet
within this latitude he will cast aside effects which

he finds pleasing if they contain a slight flaw. He
views his project modestly: 'It's like a juggling act', he
explains,—'we were here week after week proofing
and proofing; then I could *feel* I had organised the
elements'. He listed the disappointments that occured:
'Carnations did not pull. The paste separated from
the liquid—so carnations are out . . . Let's see what
else . . . Certain brands of mustard turned to dust,
and chicory syrup similarly. A cream was not very
satisfactory because it left slimy deposit. It's very
difficult to look at colours and guess what they will
turn out like. Tomato paste, for instance, dries to
grey dust. For one reason or another I just rejected
it because there were six prints; but I kept it to refer
to. Also pastels on paper give effects which I don't
like. A lot of bother went into simply finding the
results of printing'. Yet even in listing these apparent failures he was intoxicated by the event, by the
sense of discovery. He followed by explaining the
full title of the project: *News, Mews, Pews, Brews,
Stews & Dues.* The fact of being in London dictated
the title: 'England's the only country that has
Mews; and it also sounds very English. It's awful
you see just to say it; the full six words that is. It
has a corny and irritating sound to it. Language gets
into my work. Country gets into my work. The type
style relates to England; its an Old English type set'.
The most striking thing about Ruscha was the fever-
ish delight of his response to London: 'Greens here
are very beautiful. The green of Hyde Park I noticed
immediately coming over on the 'plane. And the
greens here around the plates are marvellous. The
green also on some of the large trucks are beautiful
. . . I was very impressed by that.'

In view of his responses, it is not difficult to under-

Edward Ruscha. *Stews* about to be pulled.

stand why he uses a conventional medium in an inventive way; it is because he has a fundamental trust of his own feelings and allows them to direct his concerns; his judgements are also personal and intuitive:

'I don't like . . . I reject the kind of art which self-consciously attaches itself to history. I'm not abstaining . . . I simply can't relate to it. Pressures on artists today are extreme. They feel obliged to push things as far as they will go. I find that very unnatural. It's funny that—people keep pushing and pushing. I feel comfortable; that's the rules. I get satisfaction from my work, I really do.'

The satisfaction for him is in combining incongruous elements. One of which he was most pleased with was *Brews*.

'The pleasure of it is both in the wit and the absurdity of the combination. I mean the idea of combining axle grease and caviar!' He listed the other five: '*News* is black currant preserves blended with salmon roe and the letters are blank; *Mews* is a combination of egg, which form the letters, and solid pasta sauce; *Pews* is a mixture . . . 60% chocolate syrup and 40% coffee mixture—the letters are squid in ink. *Stews* has no background: the letters here are of baked beans blended with daffodils, chutney, tulips, leaves and stalks, caviar and cherry pie filling. *Dues* is combined pickle letters printed over solid pickle background.'

Ruscha's wit is essentially affable. He does not use it didactically; it is something which is combined with the 'naturalness' of his responses to things; it hovers around his concerns like an atmosphere. He does not make a distinction between 'serious' art and that which contains wit: 'Oldenburg's best works are good as art and also very funny'.

Prior to this project at Editions Alecto, Ruscha compiled a collection of stains:

'The book of stains is a kind of documentation, though my interest in doing it was not biological or scientific. It is a shallow box of black needle-finished leather. It has a Church look and quality about it . . . a kind of coffin!'

The mock-solemnity of this excites him: 'The minute somebody hangs one of these things on a wall they miss the point entirely. There are seventy-six stains: number sixty is yellow pepper; forty-nine is glycerene; twenty-seven is sulphuric acid; fourteen is gunpowder. Most of them were just applied. Some are invisible. An eyedropper was used to apply the liquids. I've done ten books altogether. You could say if you want to categorize me that I'm a Surrealist: but I don't attach myself to a label.

New mediums encourage me. I still paint in oil paint. But what I'm interested in is illustrating *ideas*. I'm not interested in colour: if colour suits me I use it intuitively . . . either it works or it does not work'.

I'd prefer my painting to come to an end. I'd be satisfied to paint myself into a corner, and then just give it up. It's not a vocation. I just use painting. Painting for me is a tool. All the things that I achieve through it become obsolete. I'm terrified to think I'll be painting at sixty'.

Yet Ruscha also clearly feels he learns through art: 'I don't know . . . maybe, there's a great deal of satisfaction through learning. I don't worry about what I'm about to do. I don't even make that a question in my life. I may, in time, turn towards science . . . art and science are very alike. Many artists work their entire lives worrying whether their work is important. They just get too involved with what's around them.

The important thing is to believe in what you are doing, even if it's absurd. Most people's rational consciousness prevents them from doing what they really should have blind faith about.

I want people to be able to look at these prints—chocolate and syrup—and see the way that they come out as important, and to be able to discern that I wanted it to be this.'

*Original text for the portfolio* News, Mews, Pews, Brews, Stews & Dues *six organic screenprints, published 1970.*

**Anthony Deigan.** *I Did,* poem and eight prints, 1969.  Etching, 29 x 40 cm.  Edition 75.

I. did you ever go for long walks
ride in a donkey cart
or on the back of a pig

II. did you ever visit a sandpit and see the sandmartins homes
play in a sandpit among hills covered in yellow gorse
or try to catch butterflies on clumps of thistles
III. did you ever pick wild strawberries at the edge of a wood
fall off a bicycle after playing in a farmyard
or see a freshly ploughed field through drizzle
IV. did you ever swim in a sandy bottomed river
catch pinkeens and eels
or eat hawberries and play in ripe corn

V. did you ever play hurling in a field surrounded by hedges
see where the tinkers had camped
or go rabbit shooting with your father
VI. did you ever dance across the kitchen floor
or see a farmer play an accordian
or have a bath in front of the kitchen fire
VII. did you ever think your father dead and cut his hair to wake him up
see a dead man
or go to a wake
VIII. did you ever draw with coloured chalks on the stone kitchen floor
get chased by a donkey
or stand chest high in a field full of dog-daisies

# I DID

Anthony Deigan

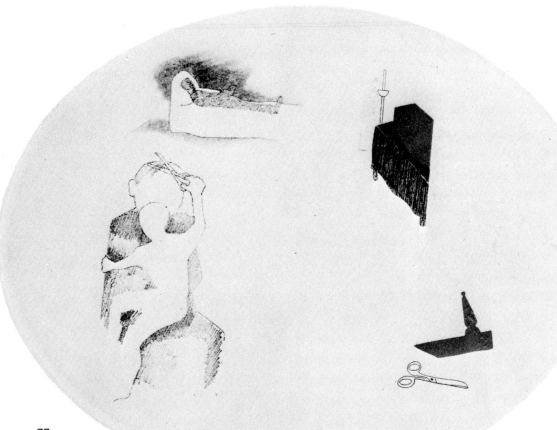

77

Somebodies old pot

along the back path
watching from the bushes was a peeping Tom
whom we noticed and whom we watched in turn
eluded and followed the path along beside the pond
coming too soon on your favourite girl

with green leaves over my head I lay down under the sycamore tree
what a strange sun that day

Toni showed and gave me some shards of china found in her garden
those were the days when pots were pots
and when flowers grew close to the ground
when the word spread of that afternoon
it was decided that our hero would not be going to heaven

but as our hero walked along the path unperturbed
pointing and saying look at that
among the gooseberry bushes somethings shining brightly
thats no rose cottage
wash off the dirt its all hand drawn
and quite beautiful a jewel in the darkness

ah I never like anything

I 13/25                                                                        ADeigan'68

**Anthony Deigan.** *Somebody's Old Pot,* poem and nineteen prints, 1968.  Etching, 22 × 27 cm. Edition 25.

## ROCK PAINTINGS OF THE TASSILI N'AJJER
Peter D. Carr

### The Geography of the Tassili n'Ajjer

The great sandstone massif of the Tassili n'Ajjer is situated to the North-East of the Hoggar Mountains. Five hundred miles long, between thirty and forty wide, and shaped like a gigantic crocodile it stretches from Amguid, two hundred and fifty miles North of Tamanrasset, curving down across the frontier of Algeria and the Niger Republic to the Plateau of Djado from where a thin tail of flat rocky hillocks drops South to the Bilma sand-sea. The central part of the main massif consists of a plateau set above a sandstone escarpment on the West side whose cliffs rise sheer to between 1600 and 2300 feet above the surrounding desert. Some ten miles from their base lies the Oasis of Djanet from where an ancient camel-track winds up the Col Tafalalet, crosses the plateau and drops down to Ghat just over the Libyan border sixty miles East. The Tassili is composed of a homogeneous mass of friable sandstone and stratified schists, and only towards the base of the cliffs does one find a foundation of different strata containing wide variety of quartz and mica. Tassili in the Tuareg languages means Plateau of the Rivers, though dried up valleys are the only evidence today that water flowed in abundance over two thousand years ago. The only inhabitants now are a few Tuareg nomads who live on a meagre diet of lizards, rock hyrax and camel or goat's milk. Occasional gazelle and mouflon are seen, while in the summer months scorpions and deadly horned vipers thrive in the hot sand.

### The Discovery of the Tassili Rock Paintings

The Oued Djerat in the Northern Tassili is a canyon leading off the upper reaches of the valley of Ighargharen, the mouth of which lies ten miles south of Fort Polignac. It was in 1933 that Lt. Brenans leading a detachment of the French Foreign Legion up this canyon, became the first European to set eyes on what (together with later discoveries further South) is the greatest display of prehistoric rock painting yet known. Brenans, excited by his discovery, spent the years before the war searching the length and breadth of the Tassili for further sites and making innumerable sketches of the paintings he found. He was joined by the famed Saharan traveller Henri Lhote and their exploration eventually culminated in Lhote's ambitious expedition in 1956-7 when, with the assistance of a team of French artists, more than eight hundred designs were traced and gouache reproductions made in situ. It is sad that Brenans, due to join the expedition, died unexpectedly shortly before the party left for the Tassili. The work took eighteen months to complete in the face of harsh extremes of climate and in lonely and inhospitable terrain. Simulating the rock surface on cartridge paper the aim was to reproduce every painting discoverable with the colour and freshness of their first creation. They show the primitive art in its supposed original newness rather than with present wear and tear of millenia. The present etchings are intended to convey a sense of the latter. The Lhote collection is now in the Musée de L'Homme in Paris.

### Natural Background of the Paintings

The Tassili paintings give direct and vivid proof of the life the Sahara once enjoyed before gradual climatic changes reduced it to the wilderness of to-day. Dry wadis were once a net-work of rivers and there were extensive forests and even as late as Roman times vestiges of this green paradise lingered on defying the heat and desiccation of the soil. In addition to human communities wild animals roamed, including elephant, buffalo, hippopotamus and rhinoceros, examples of which are painted in a variety of styles on the rock shelters. The arranging and dating of styles is speculative and one reads caution in the figures the specialists suggest. Lhote maintains the most primitive period is early Neolithic when the Bubulus (the extinct African wild buffalo) was hunted by men armed with bows and arrows, as some designs so graphically show. Then follows a succession of styles leading up to what Lhote termed the Bovidian phase when nomads and cattle inhabited the plateau. This succession covers nearly three millenia from over 6000 to around 3500 B.C. and it is to this period that the bulk of paintings belong. J. G. Laloux agrees that the paintings of cattle and hunters belongs to a Neolithic level of culture and are unlikely to be later. Then up to 1700-1500 B.C. Hamitic and Egyptian influences are evident; and more recent still are styles depicting horses, chariots, giraffe and ostrich, the other wild animals having disappeared before 2000 B.C. More specific dates for individual paintings can therefore only be quite arbitrary.

## Situation of Sites

The greatest concentration of prehistoric sites lies along a seventy mile stretch of the central plateau. The escarpment in this area can only be scaled at four points where steep gullies filled with shale and debris offer a hard tortuous climb. Djanet, a splodge of green nestling among the black rocky hills scattered in the sand between the Tassili and the Erg d'Admer is some twelve miles from the Col Tafalalet, the nearest access and the route most regularly used by visitors to Tamrit. Tamrit is only six miles from the top of the pass and makes for one hard day's excursion. But even for this guides are essential as it is all too easy to get totally lost in the featureless grey wastes of 'reg'. To visit the three major sites including Sefar and Jabbaren requires at least five days with pack miles carrying camping and food supplies, and one reckons on a walk of between forty and fifty miles, according to whether the sites of Tan Zoumaitak and In Itinen are included. The return from Jabbaren is by the spectacular Col d'Aroum about sixteen miles along the escarpment from the Col Trafalalet. There are some twelve smaller sites apart from those mentioned scattered over a wide area. The country consists of wide gently undulating areas of 'reg' terrain interspersed with numbers of secondary massifs heavily eroded and cut by narrow corridors and canyons. The lonely silence of these sandstone 'cities' is brooding and oppressive and it is difficult to imagine the activity which enlivened them in past millenia and to which the paintings bear mysterious witness. Tamrit, Sefar and Jabbaren are all subsidiary massifs of this kind and it is on the walls of rock shelters in the gullies that the designs are found. The shelters slope under the rock face at angles of between thirty and forty degrees, some perpetually in shadow others positioned to receive fierce sunlight for at least some portion of the day. The lay-out then, is like a natural stone town with streets and alleyways making a perfect refuge for prehistoric man.

## Methods of Painting

The French team washed dust and sediment off the rock surface and today the designs are clearly visible. The most dominant colour is red ochre deeply absorbed by the rock and virtually indelible. Other colours include white, yellow ochre, tonal varieties of amber and occasional suggestions of yellow and green. The colours were ground from ochreous schists in which the plateau abounds used with kaolin white and oxide of manganese. The schist strata, tilting to the surface in the 'reg' areas, vary in colour intensity according to the degree of sunlight striking a particular stratum. Those most protected from the sun are a very dark ochre passing through a range of tints to brick red, light red and dull yellow. The ground pigment was probably mixed with casein (from milk) and acacia gum. The fluidity of the mixture can be assessed according to how deeply the colour has penetrated the rock, but whether the paint was applied with brushes or with a less flexible tool is a matter for speculation. The actual positioning of the designs has the haphazardness of a wall covered in casual graffiti - some crowded, some isolated, some single figures, some large groups. Sizes vary from miniatures an inch or two high to the *Great God of Sefar,* a giant reaching nearly eighteen feet, but the mean average is probably between one and three feet. Sometimes as many as three or more paintings are overlaid, a curious thing as there is no shortage of drawing space and one concludes that the people of one culture had no particular respect for the talents of an earlier age. This abandon seems to suggest that painting for these primitive people was something to be enjoyed, a divertissement perhaps after a day's hunting. Much has been written on the subject of religious significance, but though some paintings depict what seem to be gods, devils and initiation rites there is only occasionally a feeling of their art being a holy mystique in its own right.

## The Tassili Etchings

It is the occasional brilliant fusion of simplicity and line in the work of these primitive artists which has so far remained unstressed; so that these prints are a kind of brief precis of the graphic world of Saharan prehistory. In contrast to such frequented sites as Altamira and Lascaux only a few people can hope to reach the Tassili and see for themselves. This, coupled with the fact that only a few repeated samples tend to appear in books, give these prints an added significance apart from their appealing decorative qualities as fine art pictures; for I went out of my way to trace small isolated figures generally overlooked by the photographer or copier. Terence Millington has engraved this series of colour etchings interpreting my notes, tracings and master-copy line drawings into the fine print media. It has been a happy and fascinating collaboration. Avoiding any attempt to simulate colour photography the prints convey a feeling of antiquity, while the colour and texture seek to underline the mood of the paintings in their original environment. All images are actual size with the exception of the giraffe, reduced by a third to fit the plate. Let it be finally emphasized then that these etchings are not presented as mere clinical archeological documents but as a twentieth century artist's evocation of prehistoric man's visual sensibilities.

*Original text for the portfolio of 10 etchings by Terence Millington, from tracings taken from the rock surface by Peter D. Carr. Published 1969.*

**Terence Millington** and **Peter Carr.** *Group of Oxen 3500 B.C.,* 1969. Etching 24.5 x 46.7. Edition 75.

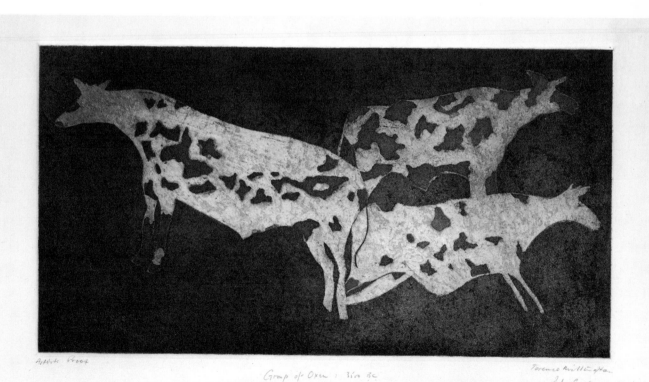

**Eduardo Paolozzi.** *CARPENTER* from *The Conditional Probability Machine,* 1970. Etching 57 x 39 cm.
One of twenty four images in a boxed edition complete with one cancelled plate.  Edition 24.

# THE CONDITIONAL PROBABILITY MACHINE
Diane Kirkpatrick

*The Conditional Probability Machine* presents the new surrealism of life in the present. These 24 prints encapsulate something of the myth, the magic, the wonder and the menace of human existence as it is increasingly linked to the technological world. The four groups of images reflect some of the recent changes in man's attitude toward his relationship to the machine. In *Secret of Life,* man regards himself as a machine (cybernetics) and also sees himself as the site of fantastic physiological dramas (Romanticism, Symbolism, Surrealism). In *From Genot to UNIMATE,* the machine amplifies man or replaces him. *Manikins for Destruction* show some of the heterogeneous 'stand-ins' for man used as tools to gain knowledge for the future. With *Pages from The Aerospace Medical Library,* man and animal become part of the testing equipment.

Paolozzi has always collected images which struck him as potent metaphors of modern life. Consistently he has experimented with ways to use them in his work. Many become part of slide lectures, films, books and screenprints. Some eluded such translation, needing a straight presentation which yet could isolate, transmute and focus them. In July 1970 Paolozzi saw some prints which Gordon House had made using a commercial etching process. The possibilities of adapting this medium to his own work excited Paolozzi and he asked House to work with him on transforming two images - a robot and the interior of a rocket assembly plant - into etchings. The resulting prints encouraged Paolozzi to explore further.

He had just completed *General Dynamic F.U.N.* at Editions Alecto. He mentioned his interest in the commercial etching process to Lyn Haywood at Alecto. Haywood proposed making etchings of some of the *G.D.F.* images, using screen-printed resists and 80-and 100-line half-tone screens. The results did not have enough precision for Paolozzi. A commercial etching firm was needed. Central Etching Service Ltd of London agreed to adapt their powderless-etch method (used primarily for planographic printing) to make the intaglio plates Paolozzi wanted.

A long series of experiments followed. Three different plates were made from a picture of a toy robot commando. Each plate was etched to a different depth

and different sized half-tone screens were used. Much was learned, but none of the prints were acceptable for Paolozzi's purposes. The head of a jet pilot was tried with a very deep etch. The result was promising but the textures were too distorted. The plate of a NASA space exhibit provided many clues about scale of image and the use of words.

All the research and experimentation finally gelled in a print of an astronaut-robot. The source was a photograph of one of the toy robots in Paolozzi's collection, taken by Norman Cottrell of Ipswich to the artist's specifications. Since his student days, Paolozzi has been intrigued by the power of tiny Rembrandt and Durer prints. He deliberately ordered the robot image reduced to the smallest scale he felt would be effective. The plate was then cropped to give a tight inner 'field' within the total sheet.

The complete success of the robot print led to plans for the present portfolio of etchings. In selecting images, Paolozzi began exploring the mysterious effect of pairing certain images to heighten their impact. In *The Moment of Conception (Secret of Life),* the male and female reproductive organs rest side by side in a poetic symbol of actual union. The two views of the decompression chamber *(Pages from The Aerospace Medical Library)* focus on the hard-soft qualities of the partnership between living organism and machine. The twin image of the M.I.R.A. test dummy *(Manikins for Destruction)* makes a poignant play on 'before and after' advertising. The Mouse/Coca-Cola print *(Pages from The Aerospace Medical Library)* suggests a different 'before and after' theme as the vanishing Coke and its accompanying time-table reverberate against the results of an experiment which might have taken place during the measured moments.

The transformation of each image into its etching was carefully controlled at all stages of the process. The scale and composition of each print was carefully planned by the artist. At Central Etching, each image was photographically copied to its specified size through the designated half-tone screen. A positive was made from each negative which completed the translation of the tones of the original into a series of dots (more dots in the dark areas and fewer dots in the light sections). The positive was contact-printed onto a copper plate covered with a photo-sensitive lacquer. Wherever the light hit the plate, the lacquer hardened into an acid-resistant coat. In the unexposed areas (wherever there were dots) the lacquer remained soft. The soft lacquer was washed away and the plate was etched in a special-formula iron-perchloride, which allowed as deep an etch as required while holding the shape of the dots. The deeper the dots, the more ink each would retain during printing, so the depth of etch was carefully calculated in each case. A very deep etch produced a curious reversal which was exploited in some of the prints: when black areas were deeply bitten, the hand-wiping during printing lifted the ink completely out of the cavities, producing white areas and giving a pseudo-solarization effect. The plates were printed in the traditional method using damp paper, hand-wiped plates and a standard star press so the utmost control could be exercised at this final stage.

*Secret of Life* presents the human body in mechanistic terms seen through a veil of fantasy. The images come from *The Secret of Life: The Human Machine and How it Works,* a book given to Paolozzi in Paris in 1948 by Peter Watson (co-editor of *Horizon* which published the first article on Paolozzi's work). The book embodied the intellectual climate of the 40s in its blend of surrealist ideas and more scientific mechanical visions. Paolozzi's own work at this time, with its simultaneously organic and machined appearance, reflected his interest in the Surrealists' blending of fascination about man's relationship to the machine with a feeling for the mysteries of nature and man's psyche.

The images in *Secret of Life* generate the same hermetic mixture. *Reproduction, Moment of Conception* and *Hazardous Journey* deal with the secret of physical life and the miracle of procreation. *Bird* and *Conception Through Impression* consider the marvellous operation of man's senses in touch with his environment. *Inside the Brain* concerns the mystery of the creative thought-life of man. The artistic style of the images varies. The procreation trio is conceived as a series of surreal landscapes, almost Dali-esque in their dynamic visualization of the beginning of human life. The two sensory prints turn the world of perception into machine environments which evoke the realm of Magritte. *Inside the Brain* combines the two styles, presenting a section of organic landscape which is also simultaneously a detail of an electronic computer and the face-head of a giant robot-baboon.

*From Genot to UNIMATE* explores the robot world. Humanoid robot images abound in the Paolozzi

archives (one even appeared in the slide talk he gave in 1952 at the ICA). A large proportion are the giant robot soldiers whose captive destructive power fascinates modern adult and child alike. *Genot* is an early ancestor of more futuristic fighters like the robot commando, captained by a child who seems himself a toy manikin, or the parade 'robot', transformed here by deep etch into an apocalyptic vision of a giant mechanical warrior with blazing gun in a flaming city street. The humanoid robot *Sim One* belongs to the more peaceful surreality of biomedical engineering. He is a teaching tool - a tireless, accurate, infinitely resurrectable 'patient' for budding anaesthesiologists to practice on.

In recent years an increasing number of non-humanoid robots have been developed to amplify man's abilites by operating symbiotically with him. Paolozzi's image collection here ranges from prosthetic limbs to some of the new devices which repeat and magnify the movements of a distant operator at the master controls. The physical interlinking of man and machine inspired Paolozzi's series of drawings and sculptures in the 50s in which man and his tools (camera, glasses, horn,car, etc.) were physically inseparable. Many of the recent non-humanoid robots become presences in their own right. The quality of machine personality is blatantly projected in the miniature drama of *UNIMATE's* arm delicately embracing the egg with a face on it, and the walking machine is easily seen as a modern steed prancing up on a pile of logs with the human operator almost unnoticed inside its belly.

*Manikins for Destruction* are used in car-crash research by the automotive industry. Crash images appeared throughout the 50s in Paolozzi's archives; in 1964 he produced his *Crash* sculpture as one expression of the motif. Recently he has been gathering data of crash research with emphasis on the special devices developed to gather data. Not surprisingly,most of the machines simulate the human body. The earliest dummies were used to test ejection seats and parachutes for high-altitude flying. They were soon adopted for vehicle crash research. The dummies vary from simple hard torsos (used to test seat-belt restraint) to complex human simulators filled with measuring equipment.

Originally much information could be gathered only from organic bodies. Human corpses and living experimental animals have been used to collect information. Manikins increasingly have replaced organic subjects for many reasons, including their easy re-usability and their more ready acceptance by the public. Research has produced increasingly sophisticated dummies. Great care is taken to make them correspond anthropomorphically *and* anthropometrically to representative human specimens. Movements must reproduce those the human frame would make in crash situations. New substances simulate the response to crash forces of human skin, viscera, tissue and bone. There has also been a continuous attempt on the part of the designers to imitate the details of external human appearance: ears, veins on the backs of hands, a pleasant face, etc. This produces a certain poignant effect when one sees a dummy with its flesh unzipped or its face removed to expose the machinery within. It also lends a horrible sense of reality to the actual crashes.

*Pages from The Aerospace Medical Library* illustrates the transition from using the human body as a prototype for an engineering tool to using the human body as part of an experimental instrument. The tape dummy is a simple human subsitute to test adequate seating motion space in high-altitude and aerospace design. *Carpenter* is a pilot's tool which cannot be separated from its user, for even when empty it inescapably evokes the man for whom it was created.

Aerospace medicine, even more than crash research needs live subject response in situations so dangerous that death is probable if not predictable. In such tests, animals are used. The mouse, the decompression-chamber monkey and the anaesthetised baboon on the deceleration sled are necessary victims is the quest for information which ultimately will protect human life.

In *Electrodes Etc. Arm Support Etc.,* man becomes part of the measuring research machinery. As in *Secret of Life,* this is physiology as adventure. However, the focus is no longer on individual 'inscapes'. One man now is a unit standing in for all men. Voluntarily he submerges his individuality to help gather data for the good of future men. This attitude is a curious parallel in science to the trend in contemporary popular thought which sees man as a small mote in the total schemata of eternity.

The literature of crash research and aerospace medicine is filled with poetry created by the precise re-use of existing language and the invention of new words to describe details of the work. The laymen cannot help but conjure with phrases like 'pressure transducer' , 'axis of vibration', 'motion artifact'and 'output of the smoothing circuits'. Paolozzi has a large collection of this literature. He is intrigued by the possibilities of the 'language'. In the near future, it too will appear in his work.

*Reprinted from* Studio International *March 1971, by permission.*

**Eduardo Paolozzi.** *UNTITLED (Decompression Pair)* from *The Conditional Probability Machine.*

**Robert Gordy.** *Golden Days* from the suite of six prints, 1970.
Screenprint, 84 x 64 cm.

**Robert Gordy.** *Water Babies* from the suite *Golden Days*
Screenprint, 84 x 64 cm.

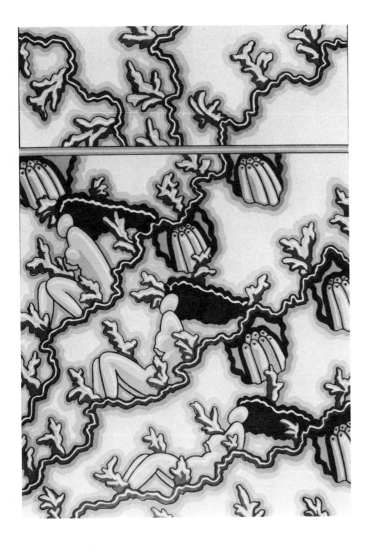

# GOLDEN DAYS
Robert Gordy

When I first thought of working with the figure, I was in college when everyone was painting de Kooning. And when I started with the figure it was in a sort of a West Coast way, until I went out to the West Coast and became very disenchanted with that whole approach. The thing that really started me was that I was doing some drawings of the Palace of Fine Arts, the exhibition building, from some fair that they'd had in San Francisco down on the Marina, designed by Maybeck. He was a Frank Lloyd Wright sort of guy, around the early part of the century. Anyway he had this incredible building that he had done, a sort of neo-classical pavilion made out of stucco and with urns at the entrance. I had been doing some drawings of these very ornamental-looking urns, and I was thinking that they were like women, they were in some way a kind of metaphor for the function of a woman, full or empty and so on. And so I started doing a series of paintings in which I simplified the woman and did women and urns together, and then started trying to add other objects which would support the female form and yet allow me to do a lot of pictorial things that maybe an urn wouldn't allow me to do like fruit, flowers, vegetable forms. Sometimes, they're meant to be metaphors for the female, sometimes they're meant to be phallic. And then I had a concern with the problem that everyone else is concerned with; how to paint on a flat surface after Cézanne.

For a long time I tried to paint these things like Cézanne - like Cézanne through Jasper Johns - you know how he'll handle the paint in that almost Cézannesque way. Of course it was impossible, it was just a ridiculous way to paint. So about three years ago, I started doing this business of step up of values - step up, step down, either in intensity of colour or in light/dark, in value. All of a sudden I found a way to fit everything in. This is like you're decorating the top of a cake and you're placing all the almonds and glazed fruit. So all of a sudden it was very easy to place things around, which it hadn't been before. Before I was always seeing them in pictorial terms, and once I found a way to articulate the things and set them down, all the images I'd been working with for eight years or so, but couldn't really make anything out of, fell into place.

I started tracing everything, Michaelangelo, Botticelli

and it was a great help because I began to understand the different ways things were distributed. You are taught to look at a painting in a pictorial way; you look at a painting and you analyse it as though it was a Poussin. If you look at a girl you could analyse her as though she was a Poussin. We have a certain way of looking at paintings, we're educated to look at them a certain way, so it's very hard as painters not to compose in the same way. And I wonder if you can compose that way any more?

Matisse is, I guess, the biggest influence on me. Matisse's way of putting things together is the thing that excites me so much. Its very hard to get everything so that it falls into place - like the almonds on the cake. They have to be pressed in or they'll just fall off the top of the cake or something. I think it's mostly a problem of value. But it's also a problem of intensity of colour too. Now for instance it's very important in things like how narrow a coloured line, say magenta, can I use? and have it read as colour, and not a line, because the main function of this thing is to give colour to the whole thing, and to give a kind of movement. And yet I wanted it as narrow as I could get it, but any narrower than that and you began to read it as line. Any wider it takes over. So that you do have to decide on things like that. That's what I like about the step up business you know, you're really painting something flat.

I've been toying with the idea of doing my own silk screens for about four years, because the way I'm working tends itself so much to silk screen. When I thought of working on this flat-on-flat thing, I realised this is a way of composing which is just made for silk screens. But I knew that to really learn to do these things the way I wanted to do them would mean maybe a year's effort on my part and I'm so busy making things that I just don't have a year to spend learning how to do silk screening.

So I think it's very important for painters to be working with craftsmen and exploring the possibilities of a medium that you couldn't really do on your own, either financially or technically, without a great expenditure of time or money.

*From a discussion with Joseph Mashek printed in* Studio International *December 1969, on the occasion of the publication of the portfolio of six screenprints, reprinted by permission.*

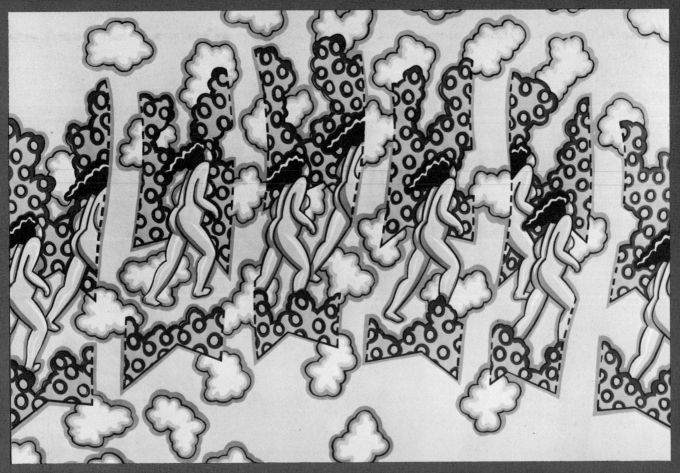

**Robert Gordy.** *Hesperides* from the suite *Golden Days.* Screenprint, 64 x 84 cm.

**Robert Gordy.** *Green Nile* from the suite *Golden Days.* Screenprint, 64 x 84 cm.

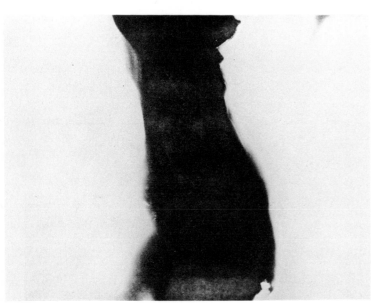

Colin Self. *Nude Triptych* from *Prelude to 1,000 Temporary Objects,* 1970. Etchings, 54 x 69 cm.

90

# PRELUDE TO 1,000 TEMPORARY OBJECTS OF OUR TIME
Colin Self

*Blackbird 2.*

Much of my work has been in connexion with the common object, seeing that every object contains as much personality, presence and individuality as a person.

My earliest works, the sofa drawings and hot-dog drawings were in some part a direct precedence to these works (the attempt at trying to draw with no apparent style or gesture in an art world which at that time (as today) was almost death wish submerged in its own jargons, isms and theories).  Also, *Cinema 14*  (1965) and the *Modern Art*  series of 1966 have direct precedence.  The idea *1,000 Temporary Objects of Our Time*  had been evolving within me since those early works and this project clicked into place in its present form and title during 1967 when looking through a book *Spacecraft and Boosters* by Gatland.  This book had recorded every known space shot.  Part of the text recorded the estimated life span of the satellites in orbit. One that impressed me said, 'estimated life span 10,000 years . . . .' which, after my initial amazement in such a consumer age, slowly suggested that it too, was only temporary.  Then other objects, everything, I began to see under this new light.  To one, a large fossil (70 to 80,000,000 years old) I have the same reaction. And in harmony with these slower temporary objects faster fleeting temporary objects whose life-span was a few moments.  Lifespan.  So slowly, the *1,000 Temporary Objects of Our Time*  is growing. I make the pictures without direct handwork or physical contact with the paper, trying to eliminate

calligraphic gesture completely, which I increasingly saw as stopping the viewer from seeing what is to be seen.

My project is like making a census of so many things (which are all only extensions of ourselves anyway - pliers superhands, corn to become or help the production of future body cells, etc., etc.)

1,000 is the very minimum number I felt I needed to get away from what I call the 'European Story Ethic' pattern of comprehension (beginning, middle, end; hero, focus, highlight drama, etc.), and to get away from the emotional reactions that accompany it.

Perhaps *1,000 Temporary Objects of Our Time*  is a personal reshuffle, re-examination of attitude.

1,000, I felt, was too big a number for me to have a subject anymore.  (Which originally I never knew I had but which has subsequently, naturally, been forced on me by the latent and growing awareness of others and myself.)  With 1,000 I felt that once more I'm a don't knower.

The following extracts are from notes I've made through the past few years while working on  *1,000 Temporary Objects of Our Time.*

The images are designed to give a legendary picture of the objects we create and use, inherit and live with, cast aside.

To show the wake of the giant ship - but never the ship.

Like the fish that always gets away.  Like the altar that must never be touched.  Like Kafka's administrators.  Like the detective who has to make a full picture from fingerprints, pieces of hair and skin under fingernails, and footprints.  They are directly about the objects.

The function of an object?
Polyfunction.
Ambiguity of objects.

Mysterious, like images that American claims to 'think' into a camera.

Negative,  Non-being.

Anonymous look photographic.

Like the shadows of people, left on the wall at Hiroshima, but no people.

Hope to bathe our surrounding objects in a cryptic light.
Remind me of the infra-red photos taken of where people have previously been sitting. They make a picture of the warmer ground in the shape of that person.

Ghostly after image X-ray see through.

These are studies of a transformed viewpoint (changed world) or new metamorphosis (world) as left to me by the graded outlines and the masses of the objects. Comparable in some way, perhaps with the new or changed world (metamorphosis) as seen through the invention of the microscope. — Metamorphosis.

Images not appearing to be physically real — touchable. Like when one sees an after image of an object that has burned itself on the mind apparently on the eye.

The 'photograph' left on the woman's arm after the Hiroshima blast. Rays penetrated more through certain colours of the pattern on her blouse than others - leaving a picture.

Should really be 1,000,000,000,000,000,000,000, (to infinity) objects of our time, of the world. The complete world, changing, transformation, sensory, experience.

The exhibition (I hope one day) will be the work of art. The single drawings, 2D studies, sculptures that survive after the exhibition finishes will be the remaining traces of the work of art.

The show - like walking into a new world and seeing everything - to get some perceptual, spiritual meaning from an object; before our brain gets too accustomed to it, and consequently makes the object perceptually boring.

Renaissance/renaissance.

Pictures in the dark.
I've seen coiled pots made by blind people that tell me what it's like to be blind. Blind people have a picture.

*Grain.*

*Sand.*

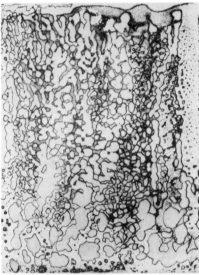

*Spaghetti.*

**Colin Self.** Three images from *Prelude to 1,000 Objects,* a suite of eleven etchings, 1970.

92

Psychological metamorphosis of the object through the changing passing of time and attitudes. Transformation of the static/complete and passive/innocent because of our transmutation. The ever changing, ever new angle.

Sigmund Freud's 'condensations' - process whereby dream thoughts become bizarre combinations.

Nothing is new except the combination.

Sensory deprivation.
They must be footprints of culture (our society) and (at) this point in time, like the footprints of animal that are frozen in snow.
From the world of the microscope to the world of the radio telescope the forms are repetitious.

Physiognomy - Art of discerning character of mind from features of face. Art - art of discerning character of mind from features of pictures.

Emigration - An attempt to make the dream physical.

Objects are what is left by incomplete body and mind; deposits of this human incompleteness ( a cup because we can't hold water). Objects are the rungs in a ladder of spiralling comprehension and need.

Yin/Yang, Ego/void, Self/objects.

Objects are oblique views of us as we turn about trying to get our complete selves into our own sphere of vision.

Like echo sound pictures - like sounding the distance between myself and objects (Myself and my environment.)

Afterglow.

Things as described by their sounds, soundshadows, shadows.

A psychological foreshortening of what I call 'the perspective of time'.
How things would look in the state of the ultimate psychological freedom.

Like pictures made with bendable light to extra reveal.

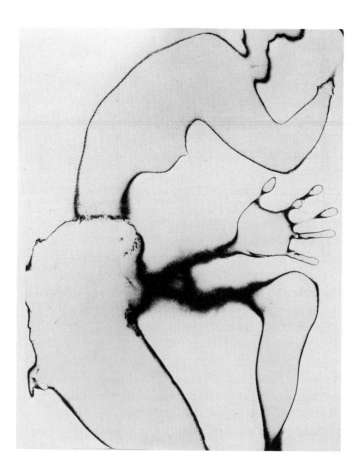

**Colin Self** from *Prelude to 1,000 Objects.*

The mental process of superimposing imaginative photographic type images 'over' the 1,000 studies in order to identify them.

Infra-red photography - One day an infra-infra-infra-infra-infra-red camera? How far back into old movements of heat energy would it photograph?

Ghosts.

Takions - Particles of matter scientists suspect exist. Permanently travelling faster than the speed of light - so that they are dead before they are born in backwards time. etc.
Takion (Greek - swift).

Violations of sivolity.

*Reprinted by permission from the British Council's catalogue* Road Show *for the XI Sao Paulo Biennale 1971 which included Colin Self's suite of 11 etchings published 1970.*

## THE SECOND DECADE
Joe Studholme

This book, in documenting some of the 800 publications of Editions Alecto over the 10 years of its existence as a company, attempts to illustrate both the scope and the changes which have opened up in the printmaking world during this time. And those of you who have been surprised to find yourselves led up some of the more unusual alleyways of multiple art may be forgiven for coming to the conclusion that *A Decade of Printmaking* is too limited (indeed misleading) a title, and may sympathise with me that even Old Moore would be hard put to it to predict with any degree of certainty what may develop in the next decade.

Not that the traditional techniques for making original prints have been abandoned. Far from it. The intaglio process, which S. W. Hayter, the founder of the distinguished Paris (and erstwhile New York) etching workshop Atelier 17, likes to describe as "one of the most difficult ways devised by man of making a black mark on a white piece of paper", remains and will remain a favourite medium, together with hand lithography and screenprinting, only lately admitted by the purists to the respectability of being an 'original' medium after years of futile semantics and the crowning accolade of a major museum exhibition in America. For the true reason why so many artists continue to be fascinated by these often apparently archaic ways of making a work of art has as much or as little relevance to the particular technique employed as the same artists' choice of steel or stone for a piece of sculpture: they offer him an infinitely flexible set of choices from which he can select the particular vehicle to express a particular idea. June Wayne, of the Tamarind Lithography Workshop, wrote recently that she hoped "the public will come to know that the reason for making a print - from the artist's point of view - is that it is the medium of choice for certain kinds of images. I would make a lithograph even though only one impression would be pulled: the work of art is the raison d'être, and the edition is merely a secondary benefit." Expanded into the whole range of multiple art, this sums up our philosophy at Alecto. Our aim is to provide the mechanism for making tangible the ideas of the artists who work with us and then to disseminate those ideas, be they in the form of a 16 colour aquatint or a video cassette, as widely as possible around the world.

In 1962 the much-vaunted "print boom" had yet to happen. In London, with the notable exceptions of the Redfern Gallery and St. George's, whose standard was about to be gratefully absorbed by the newly founded Editions Alecto, prints were relegated to the distant corners of galleries, very much the poor relation of their exalted 'unique' brethren. In America the movement which was to see the flowering of the Tamarind Workshop in Los Angeles and the other big print names of the sixties, Gemini, Multiples and Feigan among them, was just beginning, although the expansive talk of a sophisticated distribution system across the States was not substantiated in fact, as we found to our cost when an early, and successful, infiltration into the American market by Alecto failed dismally to achieve the expected follow up.

Back in Europe, Germany was still wrapped in its self-imposed shroud effectively muffling any move towards the development of an indigenous Germanic post-war school and about to start its flirtation and long love affair with the American and English Pop artists, which more than anything else served to inflate those artists' prices in the market including the prices of their prints. Fine lithographs were being made in the great ateliers in Paris, but this was long before the very welcome easing of the French art worlds' traditionally chauvinistic attitude to the rest of the world and the prints on the whole were by Frenchmen for Frenchmen. If one wanted an English artists' work pulled in Paris, one took one's place in the queue at the atelier and the edition was completed with a skill and courtesy which did nothing to prepare one for the amused scepticism which greeted one's suggestion that a Paris gallery might be interested in buying for stock - such Anglo-Saxon brashness! Some good things were coming out

**David Pelham.** *Minimum Chess Set,* 1970. Acrylic 9 x 32 x 32 cm.

**Michael Michaelides.** *Silver Reflections,* 1971. Metalised plastic film, 37 x 37 x 80 cm. Edition 250. Alecto International.

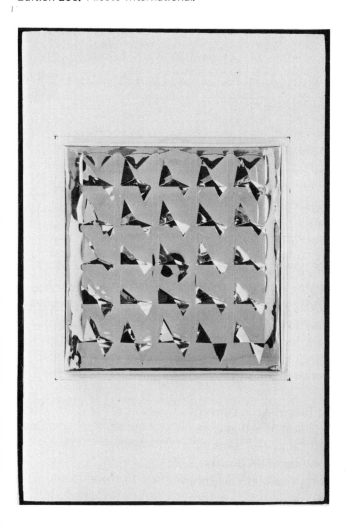

of Italy; Sweden was already pioneering its peculiarly successful and truly socialistic experiments to spread a knowledge and appreciation of prints into the most remote areas; people who came back from Japan enthused about a resurgence of traditional print-making skills; the British Council toured excellent package exhibitions to the most far flung corners of the world. And publishers and those galleries who were unwise enough to publish on their own account and to involve themselves in the administrative complexities of suddenly giving birth to 75 identical work works of art in addition to the more expensive and manageable one-offs of their chosen artists, peddled and advertised and sold to each other in a merry-go round of enthusiastic endeavour.

Since then, thousands, probably hundreds of thousands, of words have been written about the great print explosion. Big business in the shape of at least one now not very much lamented American conglomerate tried to get in on the act. Mammoth stores have staged elaborate promotions for their new found status builder, the Graphics Gallery; mammoth stores have pulled out; mammoth stores have returned to the fray with a different 'angle'. Distinguished international galleries have set up rather less distinguished print galleries as appendages to the main shops. And despite all this razzamataz the extraordinary thing is that fundamentally the situation in the print world has changed remarkably little. True there have been many exciting experiments and public knowledge and acceptance of prints has increased a great deal. Despite what June Wayne calls the 'pyrotechnical linguistics' of some Sunday papers and magazines on both sides of the Atlantic to justify the unjustifiable as authentic, there is a much wider understanding of the difference between an original and a reproduction (or to use Robert Erskine's definition; fake pictures).

Like everything else, the price of prints has sky-rocketed. But in reality the dealers still peddle and advertise and sell to each other in exactly the same way. Serious publishers, who choose to avoid compromise and to give to painters and sculptors they admire a free hand to make multiple art, still sell to the same tiny segment of the community. The great popularisation of prints simply has not happened; the print world remains almost as exclusive and cliquey and elitist as it ever was. Why is this so, is it necessary or desirable and if the answer to the last two questions is no, what can be done about it? I think the problems are two-fold, both closely

**Alice Hutchins.** *Nebula,* 1971. Magnet and ball-bearings, 55 mm. high. Published by Alecto International.

**Derek Boshier.** *Dome and Base,* 1969. Acrylic, tungsten light. Edition 75.

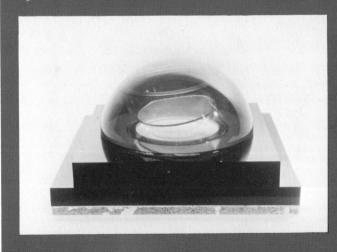

related and both eminently practical. The first concerns distribution. The second (still) concerns education.

Art galleries as we know them today are a pheno-mena of the second half of the 19th century, and important though their role in the present day art world is (and I do not subscribe to the fashionable lamenting of their uselessness and imminent demise), it is not unfair to say that the majority of galleries retain a great deal of the outlook if not the physical appearance of their forerunners. Set up in business to sell unique art to the favoured few, that is what they are good at and all too many regard their print departments with little heart and less enthusiasm - as something they *ought* to have. Worse, they retain that veneer of intellectual snobbism which can deter even the most self confident of would-be buyers. Add to this the fact that apart from the new metropolitan centres, art galleries are widely scattered and often operated in a highly individual-istic way by idiosyncratic owners, and you will understand that the traditional distribution system has little attraction for those of us who are intent on finding a way to make the newest ideas of modern art readily available in the widest sense and in a form which truly encompasses the artists' real intentions.

This problem is most difficult to solve when one is dealing with multiples. Unlike prints which, except where the artist has employed one of the printing techniques of the mass media, are restricted to a quantity which may be a combination of technical considerations of commercial judgement, multiples in theory can be made in quite unlimited editions. Alas, without the market to absorb them it is often impossible to keep the price within reasonable bounds - and as long as multiples remain in the category of ''artists' artefacts'' it is unlikely that they will succeed on a mass scale. But as a further stepping stone towards the final break-down of the contrived stratification of artistic activities, between painters and sculptors, sculptors and draughtmen, draughtsmen and designers and so on they can only be welcomed. And as a side benefit, multiples give an unrivalled opportunity to artists to extend their creative world into the industrial scene.

The Renaissance concept of the complete man, whose education aimed at a perfectly balanced training in a practical as well as an intellectual sense, is beyond the scope of all but the most exceptional in this frantic twentieth century world. In the eighteenth century the architects of Georgian Bath were probably more adept at the practical matters of the buildings they designed than many of the technicians and artisans employed by their modern trained successors who are so busy bringing that perfect city up to date. Certainly the artists who were the contemporaries of the Bath architects were often exceptional craftsmen beyond what we would now define as the strictly fine art disciplines, and were proud of their crafts. With the vast technological resources available today it is obviously impractical (and unnecessary) for a modern artist to acquire a detailed understanding of anything that does not directly relate to his own work. But as the everyday world becomes increasingly factory designed and pre-packaged it is more and more important for the independently minded creative artist to have access to and work with the insiders who are responsible for the aesthetics of mass production.

Some notable experiments have been, and are still being made to involve artists in industry to the mutual advantage of each. The best known, or perhaps the best publicised, have taken place in America. Experiments in Art and Technology (EAT) the New York organisation in which Robert Rauschenburg has taken a leading part, has had some remarkable collaborations with industry, including the design and construction of the controversial of Pepsi-Cola pavilion at the Osaka World Fair in 1970. An even more flamboyant example of organised co-operation between the art world and big business was Maurice Tuchman's massive exhibition *Art & Technology* in Los Angeles in 1971. This was preceded by a full year of free access by each of the participating artists to the technological secrets of one or more of the mainly Californian companies who took part in the experiment.

A few of these collaborations have been highly successful, usually where the artist's work, as in Rauschenburg's case, was already knocking up against technical problems in the realisation of an idea. More often the result is too self-conscious, an almost embarrassed (and embarrassing) "look-what-I-can-do" approach. One senses a feeling of frustration and even bewilderment on each side, a lack of communication between artist and company which has compromised the result of their joint involvement.

Which brings me back to the problem of education. What is needed is education (information if you like) on a whole variety of different levels, from retailer to

Peter Sedgley. *Video Disques,* 1969. 75 cm. diam. Edition 100. Portfolio of six prints on spun aluminium with motor and ultra-violet light unit.

Chic Taylor. *Sandbox I,* 1971. Acrylic and sand. 20 x 10 x 10 cm. Published by Alecto International.

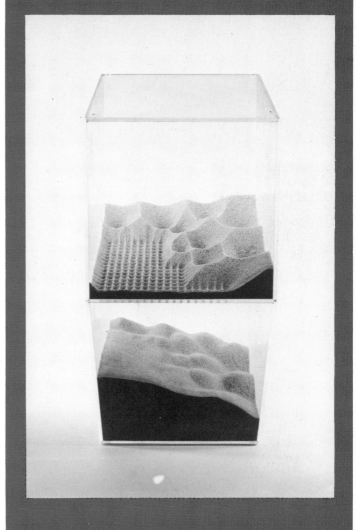

the general public, from publisher to gallery and distributor, so that each really understands the others role and can co-operate efficiently and professionally without the dog-in-the-manger attitude which so often cripples productive partnerships; and most important from publisher to printer or manufacturer so that the publisher can genuinely act as the catalyst between the artist's creative role and the practicalities of the production problems. Only if one can establish a buffer state, a clearing house, respected and trusted by both parties and able to communicate equally well with each, will it be possible consistently to publish multiple work which is a completely satisfactory solution to an artists plans.

I said at the beginning of this piece that our intention at Alecto is to provide this perfect mechanism for making tangible artists ideas which happen to be realisable in multiple form. The foundation of our activities over the next years will undoubtedly be the Collectors Club through which, with the help of distinguished advisors we hope to be able to introduce some exceptional artists and to publish some first class work. From this base, supported by patrons from all over the world, we plan to provide the opportunity for all of the artists who have worked with us to continue to make multiple art. As to the precise form the work will take, we have an open mind. Prints, multiples, films, books, video-cassettes, toys, furniture - all of these we will be considering in the next ten years. And we certainly expect to have a lot of fun doing it.

**William Pye.** *Katoubia,* 1971. Maquettes for a projected motorized multiple. Alecto International.

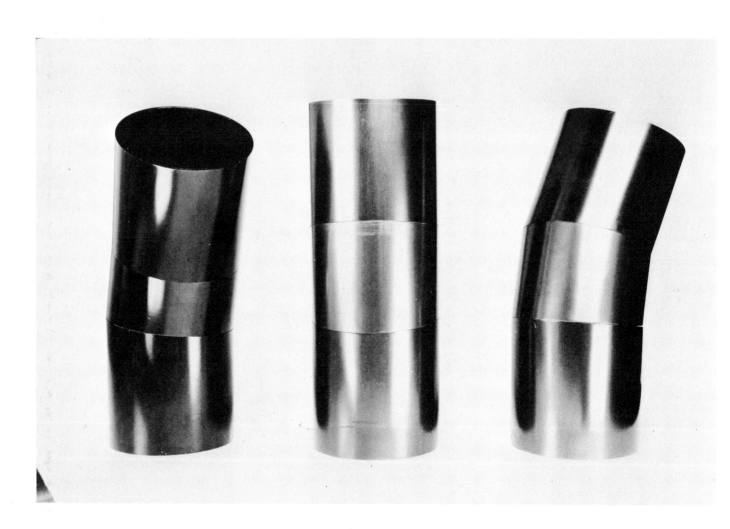

**William Pye.** *Cancrizan Series,* 1969. Metal, 43 x 40 x 18 cm. Edition 75.

**Amadeo Gabino.** *Sunrise,* 1971. Project for a multiple. Alecto International.

**Tony Stubbings.** *Windsor Box,* 1971. Metal, 5 x 14 x 10 cm. Unlimited edition. Alecto International.

Joe Studholme, Chairman of Editions
Alecto Ltd.  On the wall are Cancellation
Proofs of **Hockney's** *A Rake's Progress.*

**Keith Milow** working with Bud Shark  master lithographer at Kelso Place, 1972.

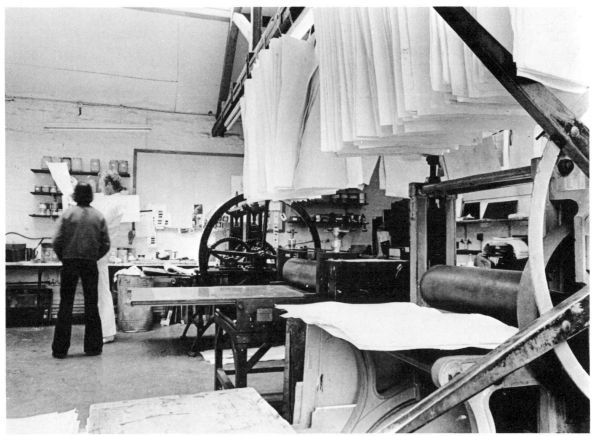

# INDEX OF ARTISTS